THE

"Pow=Wow" Book

A TREATISE ON THE ART OF "HEALING BY PRAYER" AND
"LAYING ON OF HANDS," ETC., PRACTICED BY THE PENN-
SYLVANIA-GERMANS AND OTHERS; TESTIMONIALS; RE-
MARKABLE RECOVERIES; POPULAR SUPERSTITIONS; ETC.

Including an Account of the

FAMOUS "WITCH" MURDER TRIAL, AT YORK, PA.

———

By A. MONROE AURAND, JR.

AUTHOR OF BOOKS ON PENNA. HISTORY, FOLK-LORE, &C.

CONTAINING ALSO THE COMPLETE COLLECTION OF REMEDIES
AND CURES IN JOHN GEORGE HOHMAN'S "POW-WOWS, OR
LONG LOST FRIEND;" IN POPULAR USE SINCE 1820.

———

Privately Printed by

THE AURAND PRESS

HARRISBURG, PA.

1929

M A N U
F A C T
U R E D
WRITTEN LINOTYPED
& PUBLISHED BY THE
A U T H
O R A T
H A R R
I S B U
R G P A
† † U:.S:.A † †
† 1 9 2 9 †

CONTENTS.

BIBLIOGRAPHY

Annals of Philadelphia and Pennsylvania in the Olden Time.
—J. F. Watson, 2 vols., Philadelphia, 1844.

Customs and Fashions in Old New England.—Alice Morse
Earle, New York, 1893.

History of Berks and Lebanon Countines.—Prof. I. Daniel
Rupp, Lancaster, Pa., 1844.

History of the Devil.—Daniel Defoe, Philadelphia.

History of the Devil.—Dr. Paul Carus, Chicago, 1900.

Horne's (A. K.) Pennsylvania-German Manual (Dictionary,
etc.) Allentown, Pa.

Loudon's (A.) Indian Narratives, 2 vols.

Men, Women and Manners in Colonial Times.—Sydney Geo.
Fisher, 2 vols., Philadelphia.

Mysteries and Secrets of Magic.—C. J. S. Thompson, Phila.
1928.

New Ideals in Healing.—Ray Stannard Baker, New York.

Old Schuylkill Tales.—Mrs. Ella Zerbey Elliott, Pottsville.

Primitive Culture.—Edward B. Tylor, 2 vols., New York.

"Pennsylvania Dutch" and Other Essays.—Phebe Earle Gibbons, Philadelphia, 1882.

Reminiscences and Sketches.—Judge Wm. M. Hall, Harrisburg, Pa., 1890.

Signs, Omens and Superstitions.

Story of the Penna.-Germans.—William Beidelman, Easton.

The Cross in Tradition, History and Art.—Rev. William
Wood Seymour, New York, 1898.

The Devil in Britain and America.—John Ashton, London.

The German and Swiss Settlements of Pennsylvania.—Oscar
Kuhns, New York, 1901.

The Golden Bough.—Sir S. G. Frazer, New York, 1926.

The Law of Christian Healing.—David Bruce Fitzgerald,
New York.

The Pennsylvania-German Magazine, etc.

The Pennsylvania-German Society Proceedings.

The Pennsylvania Germans.—Jesse Leonard Rosenberger,
Chicago, 1923.

Newspapers, Magazines, etc.; and personal contacts.

PREFACE.

"There's so much bad in the best of us,
  And so much good in the worst of us,
  That it little behooves any of us,
  To speak about the rest of us."

Man, from time immemorial, has been fascinated by the mysterious things of life. Not only is this true of life but also of death, and in everything in which he is a part; and not a few phases in which he is not a part.

The thirst of man for knowledge, his insatiate appetite for the things that are different, and his lust for power are common experiences. It has ever been thus, and always will be so. Man is a creature of God, possessed with His Spirit, but is susceptible to and probably often does, the works of the devil. These conflicting forces, of course, make man and his habits, customs, beliefs and actions the unsolvable enigma of the age. Man does not fully know God, nor the devil; nor does he know himself — except in part. His dual personality, therefore, subjects him to much criticism on one hand, while on the other hand he is lauded to the sky by those of like temperament.

Man is complex; has a will of his own, and is generally able to use it. Sometimes his will is used toward the acquiring of wealth, knowledge and profession; sometimes used to gain influence over fellow man.

Of the latter the author has chosen to discourse upon, at some length, for along the subject set forth in the following pages but little has been said or noted in the open pages of history. In the manner of communicating the "mysterious" from mouth to ear, as practiced by the great mystics and scholars of the past ages, we have much food for current discussion.

"Nothing new under the sun" is a well-worn saying. It applies with much force today, although there are seemingly any number of new inventions and the like, surrounding us on every hand. At any rate, we are "seeing things" in a different light from the ancients, but on general principles if we stop for a moment to read the various classics and books handed down to us by the classical writers and philosophers of the centuries past, there is ever so little to be added to the knowledge exhibited by those of old.

In like manner it ought not seem surprising to the reader to hear it declared that the world at large is almost as superstitious today as ever in its history. We might modify that statement a bit by admitting that we have come to do so many little things day by day, that through their current use, we have deceived ourselves into believing them to be just the things *we think* they are. Our use and practice of many trite sayings, in jest; our fear of black cats; thirteen as being unlucky, especially on the third Friday of the month; knocking on wood; and many others, have become habit, custom — but all come under the general head of superstition, however insignificant the action may seem. Where is there the man or woman who does not do " this " or " that," or some other " little thing," for some unconscious reason they fear or suspect may bring bad luck — or good luck?

If there is any such person, who fears neither man nor devil, and who believes that all men are created in His image; free and equal; who recognizes no evil in any man or beast, then we have the *model* man. And when *all* men, in *all* lands, act together for the good of *all*, the human race will see the end of superstition and strife.

The man who travels much, learns much; he who stays at home, has much to learn. It appears to have required a murder in York county to arouse in the minds of many people, not only in central Pennsylvania, but all over the United States, that superstition still prevails in enlightened America.

Alas! too much of it. It is believed and practiced in every city, town and hamlet in the country, and there is no power on earth — not even the law of the land can stop it, or more than seek to check it. These statements may be termed rather bold, but the student and reader who wishes to, can see it on every hand.

Until all men say there is no superstition, it will exist! The recent newspaper reports of voodooism, witchcraft and the like, could be repeated in almost any community any day in the year that any person may be said to have died under " strange circumstances." The affair at York seems to have found a responsive chord, however, and it has become " big news," especially with the newspapers, a few ministers, doctors and lawyers. It was the " straw that broke the camel's back," and since the newspapers and medical profession, and the " non-superstitious " have been pointing their fingers of scorn and shame at a group of probably mentally defective men and boys, and various writers have attempted to give a more or less half-connected story of witchcraft as being the cause of it all!

It is the author's personal opinion that of witches and "little bad luck devils" — there are none; and that most that one reads about nowadays in newspapers and magazines concerning them is just so much space devoted to a passing fancy, and lure of the mysterious. The publishers know that and so do most of their readers, but the readers like it and ask for more!

The late Harry Houdini, a personal friend of the author's, would scarcely stop to read an account of such as happened in York county because he was familiar with all phases and common gossips of similar affairs.

But insinuations have been made that there is good and bad in the witchcraft world, and it seems timely that some one sift, if possible, any of the good, (if possible), out of the evil to see whether any can be obtained.

The matter of writing an extended account of the good resulting from *bona fide* pow-wowing could not be accomplished in a short space of time. However, enough has been revealed in the following pages, it is hoped, to satisfy the most scrupulous. If pow-wowing, as applied to the ordinary healing of physical ills where medicine is undesired or does not heal, does not do any good, no serious harm can come from trying it. Certainly one man ought to be able to pray as well as another, whether he be ordained — or just plain and sincere.

The medical and clerical professions should take no offense at any remarks made herein, for no aspersions or thrusts are made that are intended to hurt either.

This discourse is solely one of trying to solve some perplexing problems, and unfortunately, or fortunately, (we don't know which), the preacher, the doctor, the newspaperman, the pow-wow man, and all of the rest of us are injected into the various problems presented.

We are willing to assume the rather laborious task of procuring one testimonial, or believer, in the efficacy of pow-wowing as explained in the following pages, for every dollar of any man's money — from one dollar up to fifty thousand dollars, or as high as anyone wants to make it! But we won't confine our hunting-grounds to York or Lebanon counties alone! In all fairness we would institute our search in every State in the Union — and we are perfectly satisfied that we could find twenty-five to fifty thousand or more, more or less superstitious persons in every State. These figures are ultra-conservative; we blush with shame when we take into consideration how high these figures might mount. And if passports are provided we will travel abroad and complete a check-up of such an unbelievable number of superstitious people that the percentage of non-such will be negligible!

When the York county murder trial evidence is all in, and the trial ended, it will be forgotten in less than no time, and men and women will go on as before — believing as their forefathers did for generations. Laws can be made — for the few — but for the many there is ever so little, even in educational lines, that will help us to surmount the barrier of the ages — *superstition!* This is ever so true so long as religious tolerance is practically free in America, and where the constitution allows man to worship according to the dictates of his own conscience.

If any one does believe in pow-wowing — who is there that dare say " *No!*"

So that the reader may be reasonably assured that the author is not prejudiced one way or another, it might as well be said here as hereafter — that what has been said in the foregoing, and what follows, is written without prejudice, fear or favor, for those who care to read. It is the theory of the healing art that has been summed up from quite some few different sources. While the language is mine — impure, and written as only an unpolished student of history and customs would write — the ideas, manners and customs you will read about, belong to others.

Personally, I am non-committal, and am but a disinterested spectator in a war between classes which will not end with the present generation — nor the next; and it is with a sense of " fair play " that this discourse is herewith presented to an already too superstitious public.

A. MONROE AURAND, JR.

Harrisburg, Pa.,
January, 1929.

————

P. S. — The various cures recommended and recipes published in the *Appendix,* or *Part III,* to this edition, do not bear a single endorsement by me — they are selected and reprinted as a few representative " cures " which are believed in by many, but considered impossible and improbable by many more. When it appears to the undersigned that most of them can be used and worked with pleasure, satisfaction and profit to all concerned, you will find more of us trying them, rather than warning the unwary of his ways.

A.

INTRODUCTION.

SOMETHING ABOUT BOOKS ON POW-WOWING.

" Pow-Wow " is a mis-nomer for a practice that is as entirely sound in principle — as sound and practical as are " sugar pills " and some other so-called antidotes for human ills. Pow-wowing is really a psychological condition.

The recent charges against several persons in central Pennsylvania, particularly in York county, as well as Lebanon county, with being implicated in pow-wow, witchcraft and " hex " murders and the practice of such " arts," has awakened an interest in various quarters on this subject that will not subside.

It appears from articles in the daily newspapers that one Nelson D. Rehmeyer, aged 60 years, had been murdered by a " hex " doctor. One newspaper states:

" The murder of Rehmeyer for the purpose of obtaining a lock of his hair to bury under the ground to break a " spell " has started a crusade here (York) against witchcraft and pow-wowism. Tonight (December 6, 1928), the York County Medical Society will be asked to launch the campaign against these alleged evils."

" The grand jury will be asked to indict John Blymyer, 32, John Curry, 14, and Wilbert G. Hess, 18, for first-degree murder. These three confessed the murder."

" The report that Blymyer practiced " black art " on Gertrude Rudy, the 16-year-old girl who was murdered on Armistice Day, 1927, has caused the State police to go to work on the case. Two troopers are now in the city trying to solve the mystery."

The purpose of this discourse is not to meddle into murders, *et cetera*, but to inquire diligently into the long and short of, and the whys and wherefores of " Pow-Wowing."

It may be added here that John Blymyer was at one time

a patient in the State Hospital for the Insane, at Harrisburg. However, having escaped from said institution, (by what means never having been learned by the authorities), under the law, after a year's absence he was automatically allowed to be at large, and restored to full rights as a citizen.

Those associated with Blymyer were mere lads, no more than dupes, with poorly developed mental powers so far as reasoning is concerned, rather than active participants in the affair.

Investigation shows that possession of a lock of hair, and a " Pow-Wow " book were the reasons for the three being at Rehmeyer's house. The possession of these two " charms " overshadowed all else, and the anxious and mad effort on the part of these weak-minded boys, to obtain the hair or the book, resulted in what is believed to have been an " accidental killing," resulting in a charge of murder.

Perhaps the authorities and newspapers were too zealous in giving the news of the murder to the world, and pounced upon the " hex " argument as a probable solution of the affair, besides the extra-fine-" flavor " such news would have. Authorities, and newspapers especially, could do that, you know. It is easier to *imagine* a probable reason or solution, than it is to *prove* a case, especially when it must be published in the first possible editions of all newspapers.

In this Twentieth Century, is it possible that *enlightened* men and women believe in witchcraft and *hexadukt'r?* The answer is obvious: the enlightened seem to acknowledge that the ruler of the underworld can perform in various ways through man, to do his bidding, and the un-enlightened believe almost anything! Many curious ways have been talked of and written about for years concerning the Pennsylvania-Germans, the Puritans of New England, the aboriginal natives of America (the Indians), our ancestors in Europe, the blacks of Africa, and the necromancers of ancient Egypt, the Jews, etc.

" More than four thousand books have been written on the subject and nine millions of men and women are said to have been put to death for witchcraft work and beliefs during the

Christian epoch!" This according to Sprenger, and brought out by Sydney George Fisher, in *Men, Women and Manners in Colonial Times.*

One of the earliest printed books, published by Johann Sensenschmidt, at Nuremberg, Germany, about 1470, (just about fourteen years after the advent of printing from movable type), is that entitled "Compendium Theologicæ Veritatis," by Albertus Magnus, author of the book on the *Egyptian Secrets.* It is not improbable that the first edition of this latter book can be traced on back to near the time of the first-mentioned book of Magnus'. The title page of an edition of *Egyptian Secrets,* current on the market today, reads as follows:

" Albertus Magnus: being the approved, verified, sympathetic and natural Egyptian Secrets; or White and Black Art for Man and Beast. The book of nature and the hidden secrets and mysteries of life unveiled; being the forbidden knowledge of ancient philosophers, etc. Translated from the German. Three volumes in one."

In the library of the Landis Valley, Lancaster County, Museum, is a copy of *"Albertus Magnus; substantiated and approved Sympathy and Natural Egyptian Secrets for Man and Beast; for City and County dwellers."* One copy in the library is imprinted Brabant, 1725, but another, exactly the same, is dated 1866 and still another 1857. This is a famous work and 1725 may not be far from the date of its origin as a book, although Albertus Magnus himself lived about 1250. He was a contemporary of Thomas a'Kempis, and was a Dominican Monk of the Franciscan Order.

The book just described above, comes usually in a 12mo, or 5 by 7-inch size. It is usually available in what is commonly called " paper covers." It can also be had cloth bound. There is no ban on the sale of the book, nor has there ever been according to the knowledge of the best authorities, and it can be had from any good book store, in almost any city or town in the entire country. Several editions are always in print, and they are sold by the thousands. The prevailing price is $1.00 a copy.

To classify the numerous items of interest that appear in
Albertus Magnus, one might as well reprint the entire book.
They are many, and varied; for the ills of man or beast.
The book numbers almost 200 pages, and is well indexed
for each of the three parts into which it is divided.

Opening the book at random, one's eye may meet with
such as the following:

To Try if a Person is Chaste

Sap of radish squeezed into the hand will prove what
you wish to know. If they do not fumble or grapple
they are all right.

How to Cause Your Intended Wife to Love You

Take feathers from a rooster's tail, press them three
times into her hand. Probatum.

Or: Take a turtle dove tongue into your mouth, talk
to your friend agreeably, kiss her and she will love you
so dearly that she cannot love another.

When You Wish That Your Sweetheart Shall Not Deny You

Take the turtle dove tongue into your mouth again
and kiss her, and she will accept your suit.

Or: Take salt, cheese and flour, mix it together, put
it into her room, and she will have no rest until she sees
you.

To Cause Hair to Grow Wherever You Wish

Take the milk of a slut, and saturate therewith the
spot wherever the hair is desired to grow. Probatum est!

Any number of odd and curious recipes and items of interest are to be found in this work, the republishing of many
of which would prove of much satisfaction and humor to
the reader. However, as said, the edition may be procured
almost anywhere for a dollar.

It should be understood that we are not backing-up any
of the recipes, or opinions of these ancient writers, no more

than does the furniture man "stand back" of every bed he sells, even though he claims to do so. The various excerpts are provided as examples which will interest almost any person.

Concurrent with the modern day use of the book *Albertus Magnus,* is another, called *The Sixth and Seventh Books of Moses* or "Moses' Magical Spirit-Art, known as the Wonderful Arts of the old wise Hebrews, taken from the Mosaic Books of the Cabala and Talmud, for the good of Mankind. Translated from the German, word for word, according to old writings; with numerous engravings."

These two books, dating their original uses back to times before the Christian Era, have been the hand-books of hundreds of thousands of persons who were believers and practitioners, as well as unbelievers of the magical arts.

Concerning the *Sixth and Seventh Books of Moses,* which is the common term for the magical works of the Jewish law-giver, we read from recent authorities, that "Moses apparently acquired his knowledge of magical practices from the Egyptians, as it is recorded in the Old Testament that he was 'learned in all the wisdom of the Egyptians and mighty in words and in deeds.' The story of the brazen serpent and the power to control and direct the movement of such venomous reptiles are acts that were doubtless known to the Egyptians in those days. Lane mentions, that the native magicians he met with had a method of hypnotizing a viper by compressing its head and making it appear like a rod."

The *Sixth and Seventh Books of Moses* is one of those books which at one time was said to have been looked upon by many of the superstitious as being a decidedly bad book to have about the house. It was originally published as a valuable compendium of the curiosities of literature generally, and especially of that pertaining to magic. As mentioned elsewhere, this title is but one of possibly more than four thousand books on the subject of magic. There are those who believe implicitly in the arts and sciences advanced by this book, while others get their enjoyment out of it by laughing at its supposed improbabilities.

The publication is not scarce, as has been stated by various writers, but is available at the usual price of a dollar a copy, "Wherever Books Are Sold." The book has filled a demand on the part of people of almost all classes and races, for centuries, and is translated in accordance with an old manuscript. It is profusely illustrated with wood-cut plates.

Concerning the books, we read as follows:

"INSTRUCTION. These two books were revealed by God, the Almighty, to his faithful servant Moses, on Mount Sinai, *intervale lucis*, and in this manner they also came into the hands of Aaron, Caleb, Joshua, and finally to David and his son Solomon and their high priest Sadlock. Therefore, they are *Bibliis arcanum arcanorum*, which means, Mystery of all Mysteries."

This book exhibits numerous of the so-called magic, or secret seals. These are intelligible to those who are familiar with, and can perform magic, etc. Others will be obliged to satisfy themselves with mere reading, or trying to read same.

The " Seventh Book of Moses " is translated into English by Rabbi Chaleb, from the Weimar Bible. It includes many mystical figures, (in Hebrew characters), tables, formulas, etc. In a portion of the book, there is a chapter devoted to " The Magic of the Israelites." To quote from it: " Having already spoken about the import of Christian healing and given more or less of a historical character, I will submit the matter to each reader to form his own conclusions to their special peculiarities, in order that he may select that which is most instructive. One thing must not be omitted, in conclusion, and that is, we must first become Christians before we can perform cures by Christian methods. Very few are really Christians who call themselves such; they are only Christians in name and appearance.

" The art of healing, according to scriptural principles, deserves special mention here, because scriptural healing is often regarded as the only true one. The principles of this art of healing have been fully established according to certain declarations and doctrines of the Bible. (See Leviticus xxvi 14; Deuteronomy xxviii 15-22, etc.; Exodus xiv 26; also, Ecclesiasticus (Apocrypha) xxxviii 9; Psalms cvii 17-20.)

"In this manner, therefore, there exists a higher medical science than the ordinary one, and other pious persons than physicians can heal diseases."

"Honor a physician with the honor due unto him for the use ye may have of him, for the Lord hath created him, and he shall receive honor of the king. The skill of the physician shall lift up his head, and in the sight of great men he shall be in admiration." (Ecclesiasticus xxxviii 1-9.)

"If a being is in earnest to live in unconditional obedience toward God, and becomes converted to God through living, active faith, then God becomes his physician, and he no longer requires the services of an earthly doctor."

For a physician there is also some preparation necessary.

"He must heal the inner man (the soul), for without rest in the soul (inward peace), there can be no real cure of the body; it is therefore indispensable that a true physician must also be a true priest."

The reader of the above book will derive many facts that for years have been more or less fixed in his mind, but which he doubted because he could scarcely find the source from which they emanated. If read for no other reason than of passing interest, much is to be learned of ancient practices, etc.

There is also included a chapter on the "Use and Efficacy of the Psalms, and the many purposes to which they may be applied." Each Psalm is then explained in full, and what purposes it may best be put to.

A third book is John George Hohman's *Pow Wows, or The Long Lost Friend;* "A collection of mysterious arts and remedies for man as well as animals, with many proofs of their virtue and efficacy in healing diseases, etc., the greater part of which was never published until they appeared in print for the first time in the U. S. in the year 1820." This book is the standard American work pertaining to the so-called art of

Pow-Wowing. The wide circulation it has had since it was first published in this country, in 1820, would startle the uninformed, but suffice it to say that numerous editions of the *Pow-Wow* book have appeared from time to time, and the sale has been remarkably steady; decreasing but slightly with the passing years.

An edition appeared in Harrisburg in 1856, how large in number, we have no means of knowing, but in this year of Grace, 1929, scarcely a week passes but what orders are received by the estate of the said publisher for copies of his edition of the *Pow-Wow* Book.

These orders come from almost every State in the Union. Thus, after almost seventy-five years have elapsed since the first printing in English and one hundred and nine years after the first edition in German, the subject is still a major one, and aside from the Holy Scriptures and the Dictionary, probably no single book in America has had as consistent and lasting a sale as Hohman's *Long Lost Friend!*

A list of the various editions of Johann Georg Homann's *Lange Verborgene Freund* or *Long Lost Friend,* (and which title might have been more clearly translated: Remedies which have long been kept secret), is as follows:

The first edition was published in Reading, by Hohmann, whose address was Rosenthal, near Reading, Berks county, Pa., and the postscript was written July 31, 1819, indicating that almost one hundred and ten years have elapsed since the first edition made its appearance. Subsequent editions known to bibliographers, are as follows: Harrisburg, 1853, (in German, as was the edition of 1820); Westminster, Md., 1855, (in English); Harrisburg, 1856 and all following named editions, in English; Lancaster, 1877; McClure, Snyder county, Pa., *circa* 1910; Lancaster, 1912. Editions quite too numerous to mention have appeared for many years, in New York, Chicago, and Baltimore. These are commonly called "trade editions" and appear without the usual publishers' imprint, and date.

In the 1856 edition (Harrisburg), appears, apparently for the first time this benediction on the back of the title page:

"Whoever carries this book with him, is safe from all his enemies, visible or invisible; and whoever has this book with him cannot die * * nor be drowned in any water, nor burn up in any fire, nor can any unjust sentence be passed upon him. So help me." † † †

In the 1853 edition there appears a second part written by Dr. G. F. Helfenstein, entitled: "Vielfaeltig Erprobter Hausschatz der Sympathie," pages 75 to 108. The word "sympathy" occurs in many old works on mental healing and refers to the influence of imagination or conviction upon physiological functions and ailments.

Several editions are always in print and are to be had at almost any book store not dealing exclusively in new and high-priced books.

Another pocket volume similar to the Hohman books, is "Secrets of the Middle Ages," containing a fortune for those who wish to follow the instructions of this Great Work in Good Faith, and Belief. Published 1881, at Lancaster.

A curious pamphlet was published at Ephrata, Pa., in 1882, entitled "Weiber Buchlein, enthalt Arsitotelis und Alberti Magni Hebammen Kunst." In 1818 Hohman also published in Reading, Pa., "Die Land-und Haus-Apotheke."

We cannot overlook the works on "Beliefs and Superstitions of the Pennsylvania-Germans," by E. M. Fogel, (Philadelphia, 1915) and "Current Superstitions," by Fanny D. Bergen, (Memoir American Folk-Lore Society, Vol. 4, 1896.)

While on the subject of books pertaining to pow-wowing, or witchcraft, and the like, we call attention to another, called the Secret Book of the Black Arts; containing all that is known upon the Occult Sciences of Dæmonology, Spirit Rappings, Witchcraft, Sorcery, Astrology, Palmistry, Mind Reading, Spiritualism, Table Turning, Ghosts and Apparitions, Divination, Second Sight, Mesmerism, Clairvoyance, Psychological Fascinations, etc. This book compares in size with others of its type, and has been on the market ever since 1878. It also sells at $1.00 a copy, paper covers.

The fifth of a common series of these books is called the
New Illustrated Silent Friend; " Marriage Guide and Medical
Adviser; being a complete guide to Health, Happiness and
Wealth." It is replete with articles on debility, marriage,
various recipes, the Cabala, etc. Larger number of pages
than the other books mentioned, selling at $1.00 per copy.
A current edition is known as the " Sixteenth."

POW-WOWING AND THE "MEDICAL PRACTICES ACT."

Another reference to a pow-wowing incident which has
just been brought to the attention of the public, is that concerning the death of a small child, but three months old, at
Fredericksburg, a suburb of Lebanon, Pa. It would be just
too bad for anyone these days to fully believe " first reports, "
whether published in the newspapers, or otherwise, because
so many stories are told on the spur of the moment, and
without regard to the whole truth. So in the case of the
three-months'-old-babe " pow-wow doctors " are *blamed* for
its death. Subsequent developments in the case are of passing
interest, to say the least.

" Death was due," according to the coroner, " not to the
kind of treatment he received from the witch doctor, but
rather from a lack of medical attention." The child, who
died of malnutrition (*obnema*—" take-off "), is alleged to
have been given two pow-wow treatments by a doctor living
in Berks county. The baby was treated first by a physician,
but the mother, upon being given the diagnosis of the case,
called in the pow-wower.

The girl-mother, Mrs. Verna Davis, 19, and her family,
with whom she lived, had implicit faith in witchcraft. So
far as learned by the coroner, J. Herbert Manbeck, no money
was paid to the pow-wow doctor, as the family was in
straightened, or poor, financial circumstances.

The bone of contention in the whole scope of affairs coming under the head of pow-wows, witchcraft and black art,
etc., is money! Did any money or other gift of value exchange hands as a fee, or retainer? If so, who was the gainer

and who the loser? The answer may, perhaps, be found in the " Medical Practices Act of Pennsylvania," P. L. 1911.

If certain members of the State Medical Board, or any physician, for that matter, should take exception to the pow-wow doctor's practices, they have the law of the Commonwealth to support any actions they want to take. Medical men are required to pass certain tests before being granted a license to practice medicine and surgery in this State, and upon payment of a fee they are permitted to practice. They may dispense drugs, poisons, antidotes, or what-nots; all depending entirely on what sort of physician he or she may be.

Those who pow-wow are not admitted to the practice of medicine, hence have no fee to pay; nor do they always get pay for pow-wow treatments, and as seldom give, or dispense any drugs, or the like. It is strange, but true, that a mere acceptance of a fee, a " few pieces of silver," perchance, places the pow-wow doctor in a peculiar position — subject to arrest and conviction under the " Medical Practices Act."

This is a vicious act that protects the medical profession, but leaves the way open to them to take undue advantage of the public, their patients, as is often the case. The patients seldom have recourse to many impositions.

It is a fact that surgery has made wonderful progress in the past few years, but medical progress has been relatively slow.

Why the medical people object to an outsider telling some one that he has a " cold," or the " mumps," or even a broken arm, is more than we can understand — even if home remedies are offered, and applied, and a fee obtained.

Read the act referred to, as passed in 1911:

AN ACT

Relating to the right to practice medicine and surgery in the Commonwealth of Pennsylvania; and providing a Bureau of Medical Education and Licensure as a bureau of the Department of Public Instruction; and means and methods whereby the right to practice medicine and surgery and any of its minor branches may be obtained, and exemptions therefrom; and providing for an appropriation to carry out the provisions of said act; and providing for revocation or suspension of licenses given by said bureau; and providing penalties for violation thereof, and repealing all acts or parts of acts inconsistent therewith.

Whereas, The safety of the citizens of this Commonwealth is endangered by incompetent physicians and surgeons, and a due regard for public health and the preservation of human life demands that none but competent and properly qualified physicians and surgeons shall be permitted to practice their profession:—

Section 1. Be it enacted, &c., That on and after January first, nineteen hundred and twelve, it shall not be lawful for any person in the State of Pennsylvania to engage in the practice of medicine and surgery, or to hold himself or herself forth as a practitioner in medicine and surgery, or to assume the title of doctor of medicine and surgery, or doctor of any specific disease, or to diagnose diseases, or to treat diseases by the use of medicines and surgery, or to sign any death certificate, or to hold himself or herself forth as able to do so, excepting those hereinafter exempted, unless he or she has first fulfilled the requirements of this act and has received a certificate of licensure from the Bureau of Medical Education and Licensure created by this act, which license shall be properly recorded in the office of the Superintendent of Public Instruction at Harrisburg.

On first offense, any person wilfully violating the provisions of this section of this act, shall, upon conviction, be deemed guilty of a misdemeanor and shall be subject to a fine of not more than five hundred dollars, or imprisonment for not more than six months in the county prison, or both or either, at the discretion of the court; on second offense, shall be subject to a fine of not less than five hundred or more than one thousand dollars, and imprisonment for not less than six months or more than one year, at the discretion of the court. * * *

Section 6. * * * The examinations conducted by the said bureau shall be written in the English language, but may at its discretion, be supplemented by oral or practical laboratory or bedside examinations, or both. Such examinations shall include anatomy, physiology, chemistry as applied to medicine, hygiene and preventive medicines, pathology as applied to medicine, bacteriology, symptomatology, diagnosis, surgery, gynecology and obstetrics, medical jurisprudence and toxicology, materia medica and therapeutics, etc. * * *

And, further, it shall be the duty of said Bureau of Medical Education and Licensure, at its discretion, to examine any person pretending to a knowledge of a minor branch or branches of medicine and surgery, for the purpose of establishing regulation and State licensure. * * *

Such is the law, and the half of it hasn't been told. As we prepare this statement, we learn of more stringent measures that will be brought before the Legislature of Pennsylvania, in 1929. Interested persons will seek to curb the activities of many persons who pow-wow, so that a preferred few may enjoy rights and privileges to be thus denied the poorer people.

When pow-wowing, or healing by prayer is brought to an end in Pennsylvania, the law-makers and those who instigate the laws will find themselves in open controversy with every Church in the State where prayers are said; not only in the homes of some of the poorer classes.

The Churches are as much interested in this topic of *Pow-Wowing* as any class can well be. There are offered prayers, daily, for the relief of the distressed. Ministers pray for individuals and for their recovery from illnesses. Wherein does that differ from the healing art under the head of pow-wowing? No Catholic is said to be more devout in his firm belief and convictions than are those who pow-wow, and those who believe in it — nor makes more signs of the Cross († † †) than does the pow-wow healer.

Every church has slightly different ritualistic services, but the aims and objects remain the same. Pow-wowing is undenominational — has no recognized organization — or governing head. The practice of it is persistent because of its apparent results — be they psychological effects — or whatnot.

The law and constitution gives one the right to worship according to his own dictates. Why not allow him to say who is to attend him when ill — that ought to be the patient's business, not the State's. It's the individual's funeral, whether he be treated by physician or pow-wow! The State aims to protect the public from " quack doctors " — but who are " quack doctors? " It is an old saying that " the devil, in full dress, is not distinguishable from the saint in similar attire! "

There are those who believe to a certain extent in the effectiveness of pow-wowing, but failing in that, they may be compelled to get the medical man for their illness. Even though he may have come too late and the patient dies, the doctor's alibi will be that pow-wowing was responsible. But is pow-wowing to be blamed where thousands and thousands of people " slip away " from doctors, for whom no faith in healing by prayer ever existed?

The situation is complex; very much so. How enactment of law will change the habits, customs and characteristics of thousands upon thousands of people in this State, over-night, remains to be seen.

For years we have had laws and laws, yet in spite of them we have the law-breakers — and the guilty ones are not always the poor and ignorant!

England still has her witchcraft laws on her statute books — laws passed hundreds of years ago. Pennsylvania, generally speaking, is living and riding on the crest of the tide sweeping through the Twentieth Century. This State doesn't need *more laws* to regulate her people. What Pennsylvania needs is fewer and fewer laws, so her people can live in peace and good health, as in days of old, before the lawmakers and medical men commenced to take life so " seriously," and to regulate the habits and customs of his poorer fellow-man.

CHAPTER I.

Pow-Wowing and Conjuring by Indians.

When Christopher Columbus discovered America — or whoever the antiquarians and historians in the future finally agree on (making little or no difference for our purpose) — he found here a set of people which, because of the country he set out to find, he thought must be the natives he expected to find — Indians. Hence he called them *Indians*. But Columbus was wrong — he hadn't found India, but he did give a name to the inhabitants of this part of the world, and later on, strange to say, another navigator was honored by having the New World named for him.

When Columbus landed here he found red-skinned natives inhabiting the land, and Columbus probably found, what many other navigators, explorers, pioneers and travellers in the New World found — that these red skins — Indians — had been established here for many years. Evidence today more and more points to civilizations and peoples in the New World long before the Indians. What all these " first " peoples said and did is not so clear — what, and how they worshipped, however, is more so. We know that they were sun worshippers, at any rate. That being the case, we may draw our own conclusions, and say that they practiced various arts — black and white magic, etc., as did what appear to be their probable relatives, the Egyptians, and others. This would be but natural, for in the history of all ages, the entire world has at some time or another practiced some forms of magic — or whatever one chooses to call what amounts mostly to " hum-buggery! "

At any rate the Indians in Columbus' time were great practitioners of the art of prophecy, certain forms of magic, and certainly most of all, what was attributed to them by writers of later years, as *pow-wowing*.

Turn, in any good dictionary, to the word *pow-wow*, and get the point made at the out-set of our discourse, that *pow-wow* is a mis-nomer, by and large, for the practice which is so-called today. Leaning on A. Loudon's *Indian Narratives* for a bit of moral support in our theory of the pow-wow business, we quote from the very worthy accounts therein from such men as Col. James Smith, for many years a captive among the Indians. Smith says in his narrative:

" Before we withdrew from the tents, they had carried Manetohcoa to the fire, and gave him his conjuring tools, which were dyed feathers, the bone of the shoulder blade of the wild cat, tobacco, etc., and while we were in the bushes, Manetohcoa was in a tent at the fire, conjuring away to the utmost of his ability. At length he called aloud for us all to come in, which was quickly obeyed. When we came in, he told us that after he had gone through the whole of his ceremony, and expected to see a number of Mohawks on the flat bone when it was warmed at the fire, the pictures of two wolves only appeared. He said, though there were no Mohawks about, we must not be angry with the squaw for giving a false alarm; as she had occasion to go out and happened to see the wolves, though it was moonlight; yet she got afraid, and she conceived it was Indians, with guns in their hands, so he said we might all go to sleep, for there was no danger — and accordingly we did.

" The next morning we went to the place, and found wolf tracks, and where they had scratched with their feet like dogs; but there was no sign of *mockason* tracks. If there is any such thing as a *wizzard*, I think Manetohcoa was as likely to be one as any man, as he was a professed worshipper of the devil.— But let him be a conjuror or not, I am persuaded that the Indians believed what he told them upon this occasion, as well as if it had come from an infallible oracle; or they would not, after such an alarm as this, all go to sleep in an unconcerned manner. This appeared to me the most like witchcraft, of any thing I beheld while I was with them. Though I scrutinized their proceedings in business of this kind, yet I generally found that their pretended witchcraft, was either art or mistaken notions, whereby they deceived themselves.— Before a battle they spy the enemy's motions carefully, and when they find that they can have considerable advantage, and the greatest prospect of success, then the old men pretend to conjure, or to tell what the event will be,— and this way they do in a figurative manner, which will bear something of a different interpretation, which generally comes to pass nearly as they foretold; therefore the young warriors generally believed these old conjurors, which had a tendency to animate, and excite them to push on with vigor."

" The Ottawas that worship the evil spirit, pretend to be great conjurors. I think if there is any such thing now in the world as witchcraft, it is among these people. I have been told wonderful stories concerning their proceedings; but never was eye witness to any thing that appeared evidently supernatural."

Observe that the narrator says that the Indians " deceive " themselves into believing their aged conjurors and their various antics.

Let the reader pause for but a moment and allow himself to presume a possible condition. Suppose the fire-alarm sounds for the district in which the reader's home is located. The reader is " down town," hears the alarm, and in a few minutes some one known to the reader says, " It's your home that's on fire! " Unless you are an exception to the rule, great excitement and nervousness overwhelm you, and nothing under the sun will change your mind as to whether the fire was or was not at your home, *except seeing for yourself,* or having later on had *reliable* reports. It may have been a false alarm, or the fire may have been far removed from your home, but you will note that it was easier to *believe* that it was *your home* on fire, than any other, until you satisfied yourself; *i. e.,* you *saw* the *truth,* and *believed.*

So different from Indian tribes, Hindoos, Chinese, and Japanese in their various methods of deliberate deception, whose masses could not seem to grasp the truth, as civilized man today is capable of doing, if he but will.

———

Much trouble is caused today, as was true in past ages, due to inability of man to readily accept certain new inventions, or to understand some simple truths. We want to show how the art of printing was first received among the most learned men of their day in Paris. Until printing, as we now know it, was invented, the few scholars of that early day had to be content with hand-penned manuscripts, etc.; the poor had little or no chance to learn anything from those better favored. Hence they were compelled to acquire what knowledge they could by word of mouth, and family heads became such as might be called teachers, which is giving them a great deal of credit. The old Jewish custom, one recalls, was that the family head act as the instructor to his family, particularly in religious matters, and so it is to this day.

For generations the people were kept in ignorance, with even the Bible unavailable, or when so, it was found fastened to its place with heavy chains.

Printing, when first introduced, soon after 1450, A. D., was so different an accomplishment, that after an inspection of some of the first productions, it was pronounced the work of the Devil; and by the learned men of the day.

We shall quote reference in full to the above, from the *History of the Devil*, a work dealing with superstition, etc., by Daniel Defoe, author of *Robinson Crusoe*, etc.

It must be confessed there is a strong propensity in man's nature, especially the more ignorant of mankind, to resolve every strange thing, or whether really strange or no, if it be but strange to us, into devilism, and to say everything is the Devil, that they can give no account of.

Thus the famous doctors of the faculty at Paris, when John Faustus brought the first printed books that had been seen in the world, or at least seen there, into the city, and sold them for manuscripts, they were surprised at the performance, and questioned Faustus about it; but he affirming they were manuscripts, and that he kept a great many clerks employed to write them, they were satisfied for a while.

But looking farther into the work, they observed the exact agreement of every book, one with another, that every line stood in the same place, every page a like number of lines, every line a like number of words; if a word was misspelt in one, it was misspelt also in all; nay, that if there was a blot in one, it was alike in all; they began to muse, how this should be? In a word, the learned divines, not being able to comprehend the thing (and that was sufficient,) concluded it must be the Devil; that it was done by magic and witchcraft; and that, in short, poor Faustus (who was indeed nothing but a mere printer) dealt with the Devil.

N. B. John Faustus was servant, or journeyman, or compositor, or what you please to call it, to Koster, of Harlem, the first inventor of printing; and having printed the psalter, sold them at Paris, as manuscripts; because, as such, they yielded a better price.

But the learned doctors, not being able to understand how the work was performed, concluded as above, it was all the Devil, and that the man was a witch; accordingly they took him for a magician, and a conjuror, and one that worked by the black art; that is to say, by the help of the Devil; and, in a word, they threatened to hang him for a witch; and, in order to it, commenced a process against him in their criminal courts, which made such a noise in the world, as raised the fame of poor John Faustus to a frightful height, till at last he was obliged, for fear of the gallows, to discover the whole secret to them.

N. B. This is the true original of the famous Dr. Faustus or Foster, of whom we have believed such strange things, as that it is become a proverb, as great as the Devil and Dr. Foster. Whereas poor Faustus was no doctor, and knew no more of the Devil than another body.

S A T O R
A R E P O
T E N E T
O P E R A
R O T A S
—*Magical Words.*

CHAPTER II.

Pow-Wowing a Mis-nomer for Healing by Prayer.

What might be said of magic, conjuring, etc., belongs in other works, and are but slightly, if at all related to the present discussion.

References may again be made to the term *pow-wow*, as related to its earliest uses.

The *New International Dictionary* says:

Pow Wow (pou wou), *n.* [Algonquian.] 1. Among the North American Indians: *a* A priest, conjurer, or medicine man. "Sagamore, sachem, or *powwow.*" *Longfellow.* *b* A ceremony, especially in which a conjuration is practiced, attended with great noise and confusion, and often with feasting, dancing, etc., performed by Indians for the cure of diseases, for success in hunting or in war, and for other purposes; also, a conference of or with Indians. 2. Hence: Any assembly likened to an Indian powwow or conference; especially a noisy frolic or gathering; more widely, a congress, conference or meeting. *Chiefly U. S.* 3. Healing; medicine. *Rare.*

Pow Wow (pou wou), *v. i.* To hold a powwow: *a* Among the North American Indians, to perform the ceremony called a powwow. *b* Hence: To hold a meeting or conference; to confer; talk; discuss; palaver. *Chiefly U. S.*

The *Century Dictionary* says:

Pow Wow. 1. As applied to the North American aborigines: A priest; a conjurer. — A conjuration performed for the cure of diseases. A dance, feast, or other public celebration preliminary to a grand hunt, a council, a war expedition, or similar undertaking; hence, any uproarious meeting or conference; a meeting where there is more noise than deliberation.

Pow Wow (to)—To perform a ceremony, among the Indians, with conjurations, dances; to cure by exorcising evil spirits. "She had the doctor pow-wow her arm, and it got well." "The pow-wow doctor, more often a woman, is a person of importance among the ignorant farming people in Pennsylvania-German communities. She mutters words over the affected spot, makes the sign of the cross, and often gives the patient relief." *Dictionary of Americanisms.*

Pow Wow (Indian *powan,* a prophet and conjuror in the New England dialect.)

Pow Wow. "A corruption of *powan,* which in the New England dialects meant a prophet, conjuror, or medicine man, called in Ojibway, *Wahens* or *jossakeed.*" *Americanisms.*

All through, whether we use the *Century,* the *Standard,* or the *New International,* we find substantially the same definitions for *pow-wow,* none of them coming within the pale of the so-called pow-wowing of today. The Indian gatherings were *Pow-Wows;* so are Tammany Hall affairs, *et al.,* but at such times, and places, little balm is poured into the wounds of complaining and suffering humanity.

Therefore the direct assertion that *pow-wow* is a mis-nomer for the more or less inspired practice of healing disease, etc., by prayer, and the " laying on of hands."

The author numbers among his friends several who are large collectors of books on folk-lore, superstitions, etc., one, at Baltimore, a well-known physician, having more than 2500 different titles in his library. Another, who is a welcome correspondent, writes as follows:

"The word "pow-wow" seems to have originated with the New England first settlers who adopted it from the Indian title describing the treatment of the sick, etc., by their medicine men. The practice itself is much older. It would be interesting to go back into the practices which resembled present day pow-wow methods."

"As to pow-wowing; it is a thing apart and peculiar to New England and eastern Pennsylvania; therefore of almost local origin. But, some of the remedies can be traced to German and English sources so that local origin does not mean original idea. Also, while it has about passed out in other localities, the Pennsylvania-Germans persist in their belief almost as generally and strongly and in much greater numerical force. The first pow-wow doctors were Indian medicine men. It took the fancy of early settlers and they said "we can do that too." Instead of appealing to the demons and spirits in natural things, however, they appealed to religious superstition, perpetuating a sort of religious sorcery mixed with anything else that came in handy, and was available generally."

"In the earlier ages, religion was closely interlocked with mysticism and magic. Today, in this country it is the religious people who believe the more strongly in the power of pow-wowing; and pow-wowing derives its power from the Christian religion and the Bible. Both depend for their success upon faith and are in sympathy in many ways. The awe of things biblical is a great force in pow-wowing. The belief in evil spirits is common to both and the conviction that the good can drive out the evil. Demons are supposed to wilt at the mere sign of the cross. White magic deals with the removal of evil and the obtaining of good only. Pow-wowing is white magic, or sorcery. Where the purpose is evil it becomes witchcraft, etc. Pow-wowing has always worked with the church. However, there may be practitioners who have used the art for other than unselfish purposes, just as has happened frequently with the churches. All of which shows how difficult it would be to stamp out pow-wowing, by ordinary prohibitive measures."

Little commotion is present at any attempts to pow-wow under the "rules" and with the recipes found in current books on pow-wows. A prayer-like supplication, sometimes with various methods of massaging, is the rule of all "healers" using this method today. Why Hohman should have called his book a work on "Pow-Wows" is more than we can account for, except possibly for the reason that it may have sounded good to him, or he may have adopted it as being more effective, in that it was a word in common use not many years before with reference to Indian practices, related somewhat to the healing art.

"Pow-Wow" appears in the writings of not too early historians in America, in geographies, the works of Longfellow, Hawthorne, T. Shepard, Elisha Kent Kane, Mark Twain, etc., but scarcely in connection with healing.

Hohman, however, collected some very promising prayers and recipes, and in applying the title he did, found ready sale for his book. For more than 100 years it has been a standard book on the subject, insofar as the " arts and remedies " are concerned, with no references to amount to anything, concerning the history of it. In that time no abuse of the practice is very noticeable, and the public has seemed to be entirely satisfied with the good which it seems to have accomplished with proper use and application of its contents.

The white and black art, which practices would form another inexhaustible subject, has been attempted by innumerable people, not only in recent years, but for centuries and centuries. This is the art that is practiced probably with more or less success, too, on so many of the poorer classes of people, of all nationalities. Many are born with such natural handicaps as we see on every hand, and above which so few rise. The many are in the same " rut " as followed by their ancestors for generations past. Some of them may be termed gypsies, some are found in Latin countries, where the educational systems of the church and state teach superstition, and in most torrid climes, where the *true religion* has not yet found its way. These peoples may be placed in a class similar to the man who believes his home to be on fire, until he has satisfied himself to the contrary, except that the former seemingly cannot surmount the barrier of the ages — the attainment of but a little knowledge, or common sense, (somewhat above the instinct that even the animals given to man have been able to retain through ages). The common run permit the wisest to control their minds, and very little *hocus pocus* is necessary to make the average person believe that black is white, and *vice versa*.

These practice and believe in black art, and magic, and all forms of deception. But the man with a fair degree of knowledge cannot understand how a person of low intelligence, and unkempt appearance, or skin as black as coal, can put a " spell " on him, or his cow, or perform a thousand and one other deceptions, that on investigation will prove to be impossible.

It may be that the hand is quicker than the eye, but the mind is still greater and can fathom these deceptions, if it is at all exercised about the matter.

There is a truth in the statement that one can, by auto-suggestion, bring about death. Any person whose mind is disposed to take up such a line of thought, in the end will be able to bring about such result. Many human complaints are due to a condition of the mind, which make one much of what he is — ill, or healthy and well. Some times we *think* of certain things we would like to have, or do; but it's true that in most cases the wish is father to the thought.

The " pow-wow doctor " of the past was not a practitioner of the various arts of the Hindoos, the Egyptians, Ancient Jews, or South Sea Islanders. He was a man of common sense, a respected person in the neighborhood in which he lived, and loved by all. He made not his living by the profession of pow-wowing, but performed it as a duty in his life — that of trying to heal, or save a life, by the means of prayer and nature's own remedies. Truly, " his brother's keeper."

Personal contacts with countless persons in recent years has nearly always brought out the fact that those who pow-wow are most generally persons of mature years, and who live righteous, upright lives; men and women of most circumspect report. There are those, however, who do not altogether measure up to this description; some of them being very much of the opinion that they can perform wonderful feats of magic, etc., of which we have yet to learn of anything that appears phenomenal. Invariably patients of pow-wow doctors will say that they have faith in pow-wowing, and on this *faith* page upon page might be written. " Faith can remove mountains," when assisted with common sense and muscle. *Faith can conquer the world! if consistently and constantly applied.*

Each and every living creature has a spirit — the spirit of life — if not a soul. Man is the blessed climax in the plan of a Great Spirit, and man possesses, according to his own *will*, a large or small part of the Great Spirit. Any attempt to fathom the source or origin, or flow of pow-wowing, must necessarily deal with things unseen.

The world is full of material things — concrete and unguessed evidences of the things we need and use in our everyday lives. Water, fire, earth — all are visible — all are necessary to life. Air, invisible, unless liquified, is also necessary as every one knows, and we feel its exhilirating effects 24 hours a day. But ordinarily, like the Great Spirit, air is unseen, though its presence is just as sure and necessary — one as the other.

Lack of belief in the presence of the Great Spirit does not prove its absence. A process, such as a vacuum, is necessary to remove air; but air is not Spirit! The Spirit is *That Something* that is everywhere — at all times, and available to all mankind. People of all classes, in all climes, and all beliefs, creeds, and manners of worship, are united on that point, excepting a few " smart fellows " and " learned " professors who believe largely in no thing but themselves!

Satisfying ourselves that a Great Spirit exists, we show evidence of faith, and there is no doubt but that it is faith in the Great Spirit, and in *ourselves*, that makes possible some of the manifold blessings we note on every hand.

Pow-wowing should be considered an attempt on the part of one person to do some one else some good — to heal. The processes or methods are varied. We are told that to learn to pow-wow a man must teach a woman, and a woman teach a man. Why so? No particular reason is advanced for the practice, but in view of the light of centuries that healing similar to pow-wowing has been practiced since the time of Adam and Eve, it may have some basis of fact in that just as man and woman are necessary for propagation of their kind, so may it be that more effectiveness may result in the exchange from one sex to another of the so-called art of healing. This may be a random guess, but that it has for many years been the recognized manner of extending the art, is a fact. Custom, which means the continued use or practice of something or other, has made it an almost binding rule, seldom violated.

That the learned and the unlearned are believers in, and doers of the art of pow-wowing, and have been for generations, is common knowledge. That results have been obtained, and are being obtained daily, is likewise a matter of common knowledge. How these results have actually been brought about is the question of the ages. Assuming that cures have been effected — leaving out medical or any manner of attempt, other than pow-wowing — we have doubts that even the healers, or patients have any definite knowledge of just what, and how, the results were obtained. It is rather vague, or evasive, too, to say that "nature did it." No administrations of any sort were made — words only, were said, or perhaps only mumbled, and affected parts rubbed slightly, perhaps, and lo, in a short time — two, three, or five to twelve hours; in some cases several days, great results would show. Sometimes a third pow-wowing was necessary, and patients subsequently became as well as ever in their prime.

In days gone by, pow-wowing might have been prescribed for almost any ailment. Conditions were ever so much different in former years, when doctors, or professional medical men, were unheard of, or were not available. In those early days nearly every home had some one or other who could pow-wow, or heal, whatever you may choose to call it. To us it appears no more nor less than *faith* in a cure — on the part of the healer, as well as the patient. The question is nearly always asked of the patient: "Do you believe in pow-wowing?"

From the foregoing one may gather that *faith* is requisite, and that with more *faith* as a purchasing power the world of today would suffer less of the grievous ills that her peoples are compelled to bear.

People who pray for what they need, and who *believe* that they shall be blessed with their needs, can, and do, with sufficient *faith* and *action*, get what they pray for. This holds good in almost every class of religion or cult. The

Christian prays, and his minister prays daily for the relieving of the sufferings and the increase of blessings for mankind. The minister in many specific cases prays for the suffering mortal — and the Great Spirit, unseen, ever so often hears, and answers the prayer! The man or woman who thus seeks relief *is* benefitted, in one way or another. Again, we find those who seek aid by pow-wowing; and they are cured! Again, the professional medical man may be sought to aid, and as so often happens, " sugar pills," taken according to directions, in a day or two, also brings about results!

Now where, of these three instances, does any one of the principals do anything really startling to alleviate the suffering of the patient? Does the invisible *faith* hold communion with the Great Spirit, and thereby renew weakened tissues?

On this matter no man can truly judge, but there is ample room for belief that faith and the Great Spirit are paramount factors in all worth-while undertakings — whether for the welfare of the body or the soul; commercial undertakings, or otherwise.

CHAPTER III.

The Relation of Psychology to Pow-Wowing.

How does the pow-wow doctor, or healer, perform his mystical feat, cure disease, heal wounds, mend fractures, draw out inflammation, etc? If any one does this healing by voice of mouth, or the " mystical " passes of the hands, the results are obtained by faith and the will of the Great Spirit, not over-looking the natural results with the proper psychological application.

As the great temples and holy cities in the Far East are not for the profane and unbelievers, so is it with those who seek the Christian religion, the pow-wow cure, or the medical man — you must have faith — you must believe, to obtain the desired results.

Before the era of the professional medical man in America, it is enlightening to the student of mysticism to learn how the people of that early day and age, kept their health. In this connection let us quote from the letter of a Quaker, who wrote in 1690, concerning the needs of the Colony: " Of lawyers and doctors I will make no mention as the country is very peaceable and healthy." There is no inference that pow-wowing was, or was not practiced at that time in the Province of Pennsylvania, or throughout the other set-tled parts of the New World, but our guess is that the custom prevailed, though certainly they stated clearly enough that they felt no need of doctors. In later years, however, with raging fevers, and small-pox epidemics, the great need for doctors, and hygienic engineers has gradually been felt, and these men are a god-send, who have their fellow-man's interests at heart.

Another phase presents itself to our thoughts at this time: What has become of the old-fashioned doctor (medical) who prayed upon entering the sick room, and before setting about to administer the bitter pills that were expected to bring about recovery? And where is he who used to pray before performing the operation that might mean life or death in a few fleet moments?

After all, much might be said of the sincerity, or insincerity, of a few who profess magical, or medical knowledge, but who do not care a single whit whether the patient makes the grade.

How true it is that the medical profession is just beginning to discover that man has a *soul*, as well as a body. More and more it is the duty of the medical man, and the minister to know the truth of human complaints — whether they be mental (soul) conditions that both professional men could cure with psychological treatments, rather than " prescriptions." The medical profession can well afford to become more religious and sympathetic, while the ministry ought to become more scientific. Both need more faith, for faith is life.

How many persons who believed in pow-wowing have been " cured " is not known to mortal man; nor how many have been " cured " proportionately, by the " sugar pills " provided by the medical man. That there are many cures effected by genuine use of drugs, etc., by the physician, is beyond dispute. How many poor souls have died as a result of the " failure " of pow-wowing, might also be a sad tale, if known; as would the sad, sad story of many whose ills were more of the mind than of the body, and whose cases had been wrongly diagnosed, or whose surgical operations had been untimely!

Pow-wowing, or the art of healing by the recital of a portion of the Holy Scriptures, as may sometimes be the case, is somewhat on an alliance with the professional life of a clergyman, or lay member of the church, who is asked to pray for the needy; also with the professional medical man, because not every case is really in need of medicine, but is oft-times treated, as if it were, in order to keep the patient's mind in a state of belief that good is and will result.

All this with the one object in mind, viz: " faith cures;" be it treatment from either one of the three mentioned.

Churches of today are more and more recognizing the art of healing by prayer, and we hear of the marvelous cures in the Catholic Church, the Christian Science and New Thought fields. Lately the Episcopal Church has sanctioned healing by prayer (pow-wowing is mostly prayer by a layman, some being church members, others not connected with any church) and newspapers currently report any number of cures by prayer and faith.

Who does not know of the celebrated shrine of Ste. Anne de Beaupre, in the Province of Quebec, Canada, where to wend one's way up a flight of stairs to the foot of the statue, is nearly paramount to a cure? Crutches are discarded there by the carloads! There, in the course of a year, thousands upon thousands of the faithful pay their respects, and before departing therefrom procure a number of Canadian bronze pennies, which have been blessed by the priests, and which are said to ward off heart disease, and numerous other ailments which humanity is susceptible to. These cures are not necessarily confined to those of Catholic faith, either, it is claimed.

CHAPTER IV.

REMINISCENCES AND SKETCHES FROM VARIOUS AUTHORS.

In order to satisfy the reader concerning some points involved we shall quote several excerpts from various sources; from books of history and reminiscences, which certainly were not planned with the idea of hood-winking anybody. These articles appear in reputable accounts by learned writers, and from accounts largely pertaining to Pennsylvania. Many persons are satisfied to read in the course of a year's time, a few monthly magazines, a few daily papers, etc., but seldom going so far as to reach on a shelf for a book. Man has become accustomed to shift gears on an auto, or twirl a dial on a radio, and has lost the art of stretching to a high shelf for a book upon which a bit of dust may have gathered. Most homes today have three or four indifferent-titled books propped up with gift book-ends that may make a very nice appearance, yet all this has a tendency to sacrifice and narrow the knowledge that could be their's, in order to be able to call off readily such as are prominent letters in radio-broadcasting stations; or whether the " A's " are at the top, or the bottom of the column.

Because of the great amount of good which comes from a *faith* in pow-wowing, if not from *actual* results therefrom, we quote from *Reminiscences and Sketches*, by the late Judge Wm. M. Hall, of Bedford, Pa. Judge Hall was a widely read man and who travelled a good deal. Please note his article on the " Stoppage of the Flow of Blood by the Reading of a Verse from Scripture." If the reader knows of any town of any size at all, in the entire State of Pennsylvania, in which at some time or another, blood has not been stopped by the reading of a verse from Scripture, said town is truly an exception, that's all! (Presuming that the reader knows " his Pennsylvania.")

Judge Hall, in his youth, was engaged as a surveyor in Bedford county, and on the occasion which prompted the preparation of this article, he had with him one axman, who was known as John Kauffman. Hall, in telling of his strange experience, goes on to say:

* * * When we were one or two days out, pretty well environed by mountain forests, John was sent with the necessary funds to get a quart of whisky to have along in case of snake-bites. When he returned he produced a pint flask full, and stated that the man who sold it had no quart flasks, and, therefore, gave him two pint flasks, one of which he said he had accidentally broken in crossing the fence. A remarkable coincidence, however, was that John was visibly intoxicated, and this gave rise to the suspicion that he had drank one pint himself. While he was absent for the whisky a part of the line remained unmarked, and when he returned I ran back a half a mile or so to have him mark it. Whilst I was taking a sight he was nicking in a fallen tree, and the axe glanced and cut him severely, a deep gash in the foot on the arch of the instep, from which the blood spurted in jets, indicating that a small artery was dissevered. We were entirely alone in a dense forest. I put him on his back, with his foot elevated, and made an extemporized tourniquet around his leg with a handkerchief and a stick, which I gave him to hold, and hastened off, retracing the line to get our party, and as soon as possible John was taken to the nearest house and a doctor was sent for. He bled profusely, and it was a long time before the flow of blood was checked.

That night we stayed at old George Ritchey's, in the Switz. The Switz, or Switzerland, is the high ground between the Blue Knob and the Allegheny Mountain; and the Ritcheys of that day all believed that certain persons had the power to stop the flow of blood; and so, in conversation about John Kauffman's wound, they expressed deep regret that some man, whose name I do not recall, was not sent for to stop the blood by repeating a particular verse from the Bible.

This idea was new to me, and I rather controverted it and expressed a disbelief in the possession of any such mysterious power, until old Mr. Ritchey was manifestly a little vexed by my scepticism, which involved a quasi censure of his belief, and thus he addressed me: " Maybe you are one of those young men that believe the world turns round and the sun stands still." I assured him I was. " Yes," he said, "there are such people nowadays! What folly! How silly it is! The world round, and turns round, and the sun stands still! Any child ought to know better than that. Why, the houses would all fall off, and the people, and the horses, and the cattle, and all these heavy rocks you have been traveling over. What would hold them on when they get on the under side? You don't believe in the Bible, which says Joshua commanded and the sun stood still, and speaks of the rising of the sun and the going down of the same. You don't believe in the Bible, which says the flow of blood can be stopped, and you do believe that the world turns round and the sun stands still! Young man, you had better go home. You've got a great deal to learn yet!"

All this was a new development to me, and put on inquiry by it I learned that among the people of German descent in Bedford county, forty years ago, the belief in the power to stop the flow of blood, by repeating a particular verse from the Bible, was not uncommon, and among the same people at that time there were a number who did not believe in the rotundity of the earth and its revolution on its axis.

The verse used is the 6th of the 16th chapter of Ezekiel, and reads as follows:

"And when I passed by thee, and saw thee polluted in thine own blood, I said unto thee when thou wast in thy blood, LIVE; Yea, I said unto thee, when thou wast in thy blood, LIVE!"

This belief still exists in some parts of the county. It is not every one who can stop the flow. According to the current belief, only certain persons are endowed with this wonderful power, the basis of which is faith. It is, however, not necessary that there should be any faith in the subject to be operated on. He may be as skeptical as Bob Ingersoll. And it will also work as effectively upon animals as upon human beings, and upon small children as upon adults.

I have conversed with intelligent men of age and experience, and in numbers not a few, who are firm believers in this, and who say they must believe it for they have seen it done. And they relate instances of divers kind where, as they think, people would have bled to death but for the use of this mystic verse. And it is not necessary that the faith-operator shall be present with the person or animal who is bleeding. They tell how a messenger had gone in hot haste and how, as was verified afterward by comparison of time, the blood ceased to flow at the very minute the verse was repeated.

The scientist would probably explain all this by natural causes — the provision of nature by which the coagulation of the blood when it comes in contact with atmospheric air tends to stop the flow, and the concurrence of time as one of those strange coincidences which sometimes happen so wonderfully in human affairs.

There is a fascination about the mysterious which gives it an advantage over the cold facts of science. But the provision by which the blood coagulates and checks the flow of the vital current, the tendency of nature to remedy the injury and effect a cure, constitutes a mystery as wonderful as the use of the verse, even if it had the power attributed to it; nay, more wonderful by far. Who gave blood this quality? Blind chance or intelligent design?

If Judge Hall's instance were the only one of the kind on record, some might doubt the remarks, even of a Judge. But there are countless others.

In *Old Schuylkill Tales*, by Mrs. Ella Zerbey Elliott, we note several articles. One of them is entitled "Pow-Wowing," and reads as follows:

Pow-wowing is still largely practiced about the mines. But when it is remembered that these healers of burns are practical nurses and experienced in the treatment and bandaging of the injured parts before they recite the charm or incantation the cures they effect are not so remarkable. In the 'Seventies a woman lived at Minersville, named Mrs. Reed. Dr. Wm. Beach said of her that " She was one of the most skillful dressers of wounds." When a man was burned at the mines she could attend his case as well as any physician. It was this ability that cured or helped the man and not her pow-wowing to " draw out the fire." But you could not convince believers in the occult of this.

Erysipelas, a febrile or scorbutic disease, was very much more common in the early days than now and came, perhaps, from eating too much salt meat. Everybody had the erysipelas then, like the appendicitis now, diseases, like the fashions, having their day. An old residenter, John Kimmel, who lived in a log house on the east side of the Presbyterian cemetery, of which he and his sons were in after years the sextons, was very successful in pow-wowing erysipelas.

The writer recollects having seen him treat an obstinate case that had defied the best efforts of a leading physician and he cured it (or it went away of itself) with a lighted stick which he held over the flaming parts until it went out, pronouncing certain words and making signs. Jacob Hoffman, of Orwigsburg, was also a noted pow-wower. Both claimed their work was done through prayer, and both effected many cures.

Another article bearing out our statement that not long since, books on the subject were much sought for. This article is entitled " Superstitions of Schuylkill County." We quote it entire:

All peoples, lettered and unlettered, have their superstitions. The heterogeneous mass of inhabitants gathered into the two hundred thousand and over, population of Schuylkill county, seems to have centered and inculcated in its make-up the combined beliefs of the folk-lore of all nations.

It is not strange that the early stories which the writer has attempted to reproduce in these pages should have been believed in the early days, but that people should still exist in the county who believe in witches and witchcraft, seems almost incredible, and yet we read in this enlightened age, September, 1906, of one, a farmer in the Mahanoy Valley, who accused a woman of bewitching his live stock. He paid her a liberal sum of money to withdraw her diabolical influence.

For thirteen months horses, cows and swine perished on his land and he was unable to fathom the cause. He had pure water on the farms, clean stables and good fodder. Veterinary surgeons could not stop the spread of death.

Whenever a witch died it was believed that her mantle descended to her daughter and she, it is believed, could cause her neighbor's baby convulsions, his cow to give bloody milk, or his horse to balk or die. Women witches had the power to turn themselves into the form of a sow, rat or cat at their pleasure. Infants who died in a slow decline were supposed to be the peculiar objects of the vengeance of witches, and many were the queer remedies resorted to effect a cure. The *Lost Books of Moses*, before referred to, and a book known as *The Long Hidden Friend (Der Lang Verborgne Freund)* by John George Hohman, of Berks county, contain many curious remedies for the relief of all the ills that flesh is heir to, in man and beast. Strange to say, these books are still in great demand.

In *The Story of the Pennsylvania-Germans*, by William Beidelman, we read much concerning the home-life, customs, habits and beliefs of the early Pennsylvania-German settlers in the eastern and east-central part of the State. Mr. Beidelman states:

Among the common beliefs, more particularly among the less informed are certain superstitions, belief in fairies, and hobgoblins, and ghosts; lucky and unlucky days; the influence of certain planets on the elements, upon which subject they have a vast amount of weather lore; belief in the curative power of magic; "pow-wow" and the like. These and many more are superstitions, customs and beliefs, not altogether handed down traditionally, and communicated from generation to generation, but most of them have been preserved in the literature of folk-lore of which the Germans have produced the larger part. The word folk-lore comes from the German *Volk*, people, and *Lehre*, learning. So that the traditions of peasants, and uneducated people, are merely the result of that which was at one time believed by all classes.

Even at this day much of the ancient folk-lore is found to exist, and rigidly believed in by some of the most intelligent people, as well as among the rudest and most uncultivated people. How many people are there who would care to start on a long sea voyage on a Friday; or go unattended through a lonely graveyard on a night of inky darkness?

Theodore Schmauk, in *Who Are the Pennsylvania-Germans*, pp. 71-72, throws additional light on these hardy tillers of the soil:

The dependence of the Pennsylvania-German farmer upon the almanac for major and minor agricultural operations, as well as for many activities of the household, and the faith in proverbs and superstitions connected with the signs of the zodiac, and particularly with the phases of the moon, is well known, and continues in some measure to the present time. In how far climatic influences are to be ascribed to the influence of celestial bodies, in addition to that of the sun, and how far the superstitious folk-lore of the Pennsylvania-Germans is dependent upon the tissue of superstition which was universal in the Old World from which they came, has not yet been accurately determined. But, doubtless, much of their implicit faith even in superstitions is due to the respect which they had for the forces of Providence and Nature, as able to control, to guide, and to destroy the most powerful of the efforts of man. Long generations of experience generalized and summed up, often in fantastic manner, in folk-lore, was the sort of wisdom on which these keen and hardy agricultural folk were obliged to depend, in lieu of anything better, for their agricultural operations.

```
A B R A C A D A B R A
A B R A C A D A B R
A B R A C A D A B
A B R A C A D A
A B R A C A D
A B R A C A
A B R A C
A B R A
A B R
A B
A
```

—Magical Words.

CHAPTER VI.

PENNSYLVANIA-GERMAN FRUGALITY AND POW-WOWING.

Men and women of today are more suspicious, though probably less superstitious, than were those of the past few generations. Great changes are noticeable especially since the close of the last Great War.

Many of the strange manners and customs current in Pennsylvania today, are found in the more densely German (Palatine) populated counties and sections. Of course superstition is present in all races and classes. Pennsylvania is no more saturated with it, however, than is any other State of like complex. The German settlers in Pennsylvania have proved more clannish and settled than almost any other type of settlers, save the Quakers, probably. Yet whatever may be said about Pennsylvania-German superstitions, pow-wowing or other customs, can be applied and scoffed at in any other race or nationality in the State. Of the most beloved class in Pennsylvania, with all its faults and short-comings, we point you to the Pennsylvania-Germans.

Count all the *wrongs* they have committed against society, if any, and all the *good* they have done since the beginning of the Eighteenth Century, and remove all of *their* record from the pages of history, and see what is left! You create immediately the greatest void in the creation and formation of the greatest State in the Union! Pennsylvania is pre-eminently a leading State only because of the presence of the German settlers who really became the back-bone and the bulwark of the State and Nation in their formative stages, and in the time of need.

These peoples, while most always called Germans, quite often include the French Huguenot, the Swiss, and a few Holland Dutch, and others whose blood intermingled. These were the original agriculturalists, horticulturalists, soldiers, (when needed), manufacturers, religious leaders, preachers and doers of the Word, Indian interpreters, tradesmen, politicians, bankers, etc. Truly their achievements are outstanding and everlasting.

Our Pennsylvania-German people are direct heirs of many strange practices and beliefs. These come from the Fatherland, and differ but slightly from practices of generations ago. Whatever these may be, they cannot be considered any more superstitious or lacking in faith than the " Catholic adherent who kisses the stone toe of a saint." This act performed by an ailing person, while on the face of it, an act of superstition, in the hope and belief of a cure, nevertheless in many, many cases, brings about a cure.

Pow-wowing goes back ages and ages, though it has no fixed methods, nor has there ever been any cult or group organization established for its promulgation. It is a genuine " hand-me-down," if ever there was such. No more common expression is heard in rural Pennsylvania today, at least where German is spoken in small degree, than *hala, hala, hinkel drek, bis morga fre gaet ollus weck!* This, accompanied with brisk rubbing on the spot or part which a youngster may have hurt in a fall, or bumped, is not strictly pow-wowing, yet it does in a measure help the child believe that in the morning all pain will have ceased, and all be well.

Withal that pow-wowing is more prevalent among the Pennsylvania-Germans than any other class, it must be said that it is not confined strictly to that class. Nor are they, alone, of this State's various types and nationalities, of the most superstitious type. The study of the folk-lore of all European countries, reveals a great amount of the same practice, manners and customs surviving their settlement in America, as was the case and belief in their homeland.

The Scotch-Irish crop out much, too, in our State's early history, and where the Scotch and Irish were on the borders and frontiers, there you found the Germans close behind. And from this nip and tuck race between these peoples, there has extended a line from coast to coast, each taking their various characteristics and customs with them, into sister and far-distant States.

While the Scotch and Irish scattered, the Germans assumed a clannishness, and formed small communities, towns, and cities, so that today Pennsylvania has any number of counties, cities and towns, where the Pensnylvania-German tongue is heard almost as much as is English. With the retention of the language, there has also come down from generation upon generation, much of the superstition that without much effort can be traced back to the Fatherland, on through the dark ages, and even to the years 1200 B. C.

Superstition, while there is much of it all over the land, does not rule, however. Much of it is harmless, and as we grow older, we grow wiser, and some of the " proverbs " of the superstitious are proving to be more witty than practical.

CHAPTER V.

Similar Practices are World-Wide.

" One event is always the son of another, and we must never forget the parentage," said a Bechuana chief to Casalis, the African Missionary. If we but stopped to reason the truth of the above remark, not much would the scientific and learned men point their fingers and scoff at the lower classes who believe, and even practice pow-wowing, etc. Considering Europe and America's great educational institutions, and great strides in learning, there is scarcely any difference worth the turning of a hand, when speaking of superstition in those parts as compared to the African negroid tribes. There are countless other writers who take the same attitude.

For in America are we not superstitious of the number " 13," especially on Friday, and more so on the third Friday of the month; we dislike two-dollar bills; rap on wood; blow on dice, and countless other little things, all unconsciously — all day long. And we do it because every man, woman and child is the off-spring of a superstitious parent, or certainly not many generations removed from such.

In England today the nurse scolds a child for getting out of bed with " the wrong foot foremost."

In Scotland " There is an opinion that many entertain * * * that a papist priest can cast out devils and cure madness, and that the Presbyterian clergy have no such power." So Bourne says of the Church of England clergy, that the vulgar think them no conjurers, and say none can lay (drive out) spirits but popish priests.

As mentioned above, we read in a book published in England in 1928, " The belief that the priest owing to his office possesses a certain power to put a spell on an offender, or — as termed in Ireland — ' to put a curse upon him,' survives till the present day." And this is one of the beliefs that the

Roman Church permits to go undenied wherever the cross is carried.

To draw the line of pow-wowing, and not over-step it, is difficult, for in research in the fields of bibliography, there is so much to be gleaned from the pages of history that one's head "fairly swims" when we take into but partial account the great and divers manners and customs, as well as superstitions of men and women throughout the whole world. It behooves us to "gird up our loins" and grit our teeth with a fuller determination to help others, rather than condemn them for doing today, what our parents did yesterday. America is full of false notions and crimes against reason and society.

If we but understood more clearly the hidden secrets and meanings in the manners and customs of people all over the world, as they have come down through the centuries, we could better appreciate our fellowman. Many trite sayings and customs have had their source so far back as to have lost their true meaning. To know more may command more respect, and to respect others would be to know them, and understand them better. Ignorance of race custom and ideals prevents uniting the nations of the world.

If pow-wowing is healing by Divine power, it might be well to inquire into the methods of the Master, who cured many persons, and who said in John xiv, 12 — "He that believeth on me, the works that I do shall he do also."

Again in James v, 14 — "Is any sick among you? Let him call for the elders of the church; and let them pray over him   *   *   and the prayer of faith shall save the sick."

It is a well known fact that Jesus was not a medical man, even though he was the Great Physician!

The average person today is liable to err in believing that pow-wowing is something along the magical line, but this is not a fact. It is not as widely practiced in proportion to the population of today as it was years ago. It has always been more or less of mystery to most persons, and to the uninformed there seemed to be a dread, or fear; even at the mere mention of the name. The secretiveness of it all has come down through the ages. Before the era of printing, practitioners of pow-wowing, or whatever it might have been called prior to the time the English and Germans settled among the Indians in America, and all engaged in the various arts, sciences, religion, etc., were of a secretive, selfish disposition. As no books, as we know them now, were available in former years, quite some few records were preserved and revealed in manuscripts. These were available to only a few. Others in possession of knowledge of the various arts, would communicate their intelligence to members of the family, etc. Thus we see how the practices of olden times have come down almost to date.

The so-called magicians of these olden times, as revealed in old manuscripts, show a remarkable knowledge of the power of certain drugs, for good and bad, and a thousand and one other hallucinations which come properly under the head of magic. Mention of it is made here to show and indicate to the reader that the deceptive arts are not a part of pow-wowing.

Says another writer: " The instinct of mystery, common to mankind, among civilized and uncivilized communities, appears to have arisen primarily from ignorance or limitations of knowledge and fear of the unknown future." How true.

In the author's business life, it is frequently possible to discuss the book of *Pow Wows,* and to hear people remark about the *Sixth and Seventh Books of Moses,* saying: " I wouldn't have a book like that in the house; I'd be afraid something might happen to me. You know some people can put " spells " on a person, or any of his live stock, if he has a book like that! " and so on ———

Is this ignorance? or can persons cast " spells? " But that is not a part of our subject, and must, for want of time, go over until some other event develops, when that and kindred subjects can be taken up.

Of the great amount of magic practiced at one time in the Old World, we have read an account, that in the city of Ephesus, at the time of the Apostles, there were large libraries with " books and books," upon the subject of magic.

Many who believed and practiced the art in that olden day, brought their books, some of which even at that time were thought to be valuable, being worth 50,000 pieces of silver, and they were publicly burned. (Acts xix, 19). This was a loss to posterity which would be impossible to estimate.

CHAPTER VII.

EARLY SUPERSTITIONS IN PENNA., AND A "WITCH" TRIAL.

Watson, in his *"Annals of Philadelphia and Pennsylvania in the Olden Time,"* says:

Our forefathers (the ruder part) brought with them much of the superstition of the "fatherland," and here it found much to cherish and sustain it, in the credulity of the Dutch and Swedes, nor less from the Indians, who always abounded in marvellous relations, much incited by their conjurors and pow-wows. Facts which have come down to our more enlightened times, can now no longer terrify; but may often amuse, as Cowper says,

> *There's something in that ancient superstition,*
> *Which, erring as it is, our fancy loves!*

From the provincial executive minutes, preserved at Harrisburg, we learn the curious fact of an actual trial for witchcraft. On the 27th of 12 mo., 1683, Margaret Mattson and Yeshro Hendrickson, (Swedish women) who had been accused as witches on the 7th inst. were cited to their trial; on which occasion there were present, as their judges, Governor William Penn and his council, James Harrison, William Biles, Lasse Cock, William Haigne, C. Taylor, William Clayton and Thomas Holmes. The Governor having given the Grand Jury their charge, they found the bill! The testimony of the witnesses before the Petit Jury is recorded. Such of the Jury as were absent were fined forty shillings each.

Margaret Mattson being arraigned, "she pleads not guilty, and will be tried by the country." Sundry witnesses were sworn, and many vague stories told—as that she bewitched calves, geese, &c., &c.—that oxen were rather above her malignant powers, but which reached all other cattle.

The daughter of Margaret Mattson was said to have expressed her convictions of her mother being a witch. And the reported say-so's of the daughter were given in the evidence. The dame Mattson "denieth Charles Ashcom's attestation at her soul, and saith where is my daughter? let her come and say so,"—"the prisoner denieth all things, and saith that the witness speaks only by hear say." Governor Penn finally charged the Jury, who brought in a verdict sufficiently ambiguous and ineffective for such a dubious offence, saying they find her "guilty of having the common fame of a witch, but not guilty in the manner and form as she stands indicted." They, however, take care to defend the good people from their future malfaisance by exacting from each of them security for good behaviour for six months. A decision more wise than hanging or drowning! They had each of them husbands, and Lasse Cock served as interpreter for Mrs. Mattson. The whole of this trial may be seen in detail in my MS. Annals, page 506, in the Historical Society.

By this judicious verdict we as Pennsylvanians have probably escaped the odium of Salem. It is not, however, to be concealed that we had a law standing against witches; and it may possibly exonerate us in part, and give some plea for the trial itself, to say it was from a precedent by statute of King James I. That act was held to be part of our law by an act of our provincial Assembly, entitled "an act against conjuration, witchcraft and dealing with evil and wicked spirits." It says therein, that the act of King James I. "shall be put into execution in this province, and be of like force and effect as if the same were here repeated and enacted!" So solemnly and gravely sanctioned as was that act of the king, what could we as colonists do! Our act as above was confirmed in all its parts, by the dignified council of George II., in the next year after its passage here, in the presence of eighteen peers, including the great duke of Marlborough himself!

The superstition, such as it was, may have been deemed the common sin of the day. The enlightened Judge Hale himself fell into its belief. Our sister city, New York, had also her troubles with her witches. Soon after the English began to rule there, in 1664, a man and wife were arraigned as such, and a verdict found by the Jury against one of them; and in 1672, the people of West Chester complained to the British governor, of a witch among them. A similar complaint, made next year to the Dutch governor, Colve, was dismissed as groundless. The Virginians too, lax as we may have deemed them then in religious sentiments, had also their trial of Grace Sherwood, in Princess Ann county—as the records still there may show. The populace also seconded the court, by subjecting her to the trial of water, and the place at Walks' farm, near the ferry, is still called "witch duck!" The Bible, it must be conceded, always countenanced these credences; but now, "a generation more refined" think it their boast to say "we have no hoofs nor horns in our religion!"

An old record of the province, of 1695, states the case of Robert Reman, presented at Chester for practising geomantry, and divining by a stick. The Grand Jury also presented the following books as vicious, to wit:—Hidson's Temple of Wisdom, which teaches geomantry; Scott's Discovery of Witchcraft, and Cornelius Agrippa's Teaching Negromancy —another name probably for necromancy. The latter latinized name forcibly reminds one of those curious similar books of great value, (even of fifty thousand pieces of silver,) destroyed before Paul at Ephesus — "multi autum curiosa agentium, conferentes libros combusserunt coram omnibus."

Superstition has been called the "seminal principle of religion," because it undoubtedly has its origin in the dread of a spiritual world of which God is the supreme. The more vague and undefined are disposed to the legends of the nursery. As the man who walks in the dark, not seeing or knowing his way, must feel increase of fear at possible dangers he cannot define, so he who goes abroad in the broad light of day proceeds fearlessly, because he sees and knows as harmless all the objects which surround him. Wherefore we infer, that if we have less terror of imagination now, it is ascribable to our superior light and general diffusion of intelligence, thereby setting the mind at rest in many of these things. In the mean time there is a class who will cherish their own distresses. They intend religious dread, but from misconceptions of its real beneficence and "good will to men," they,—

> Draw a wrong copy of the Christian face
> Without the smile, the sweetness, or the grace.

We suppose some such views possessed the mind of the discriminating Burke, when he incidentally gave in his suffrage in their favour, saying, "Superstition is the religion of the feeble minds, and they must be tolerated in an intermixture of it in some shape or other, else you deprive weak minds of a resource, found necessary to the strongest." Dean Swift has called it "the spleen of the soul."

Doctor Christopher Witt, born in England in 1675, came to this country in 1704, and died in Germantown in 1765, at the age of 90. He was a skilful physician, and a learned religious man. He was reputed a magus or diviner, or in grosser terms, a conjurer. He was a student and a believer in all the learned absurdities and marvellous pretensions of the Rosicrucian philosophy. The Germans of that day, and many of the English, practised the casting of nativities. As this required mathematical and astronomical learning, it often followed that such a competent scholar was called a "fortune-teller." Doctor Witt cast nativities for reward, and was called a conjuror, while his friend Christopher Lehman, who could do the same, and actually cast the nativities of his own children, (which I have seen,) was called a scholar and a gentleman.

Germantown was certainly very fruitful in credulity, and gave support to some three regular professors in the mysterious arts of hocus pocus and divination. Besides the Doctor before named, there was his disciple and once his intimate, Mr. Fraily—sometimes dubbed doctor also, though not possessed of learning. He was, however, pretty skilful in several diseases. When the cows and horses, and even persons, got strange diseases, such as baffled ordinary medicines, it was often a dernier resort to consult either of these persons for relief, and their prescriptions, without seeing the patients, were often given under the idea of witchcraft somehow, and the cure was effected!

The superstition then was very great about ghosts and witches. "Old Shrunk," as he was called, (George S., who lived to be 80,) was a great conjuror, and numerous persons from Philadelphia and elsewhere, and some even from Jersey, came to him often, to find out stolen goods and to get their fortunes told. They believed *he* could *make* any thieves who came to steal from his orchard "stand," if he saw them, even while they desired to run away. They used to consult him where to go and dig money; and several persons, whose names I suppress, used to go and dig for hidden treasures of nights. On such occasions, if any one "*spoke,*" while digging, or ran, from "*terror,*" without "the *magic ring,*" previously made with incantation around the place, the whole influence of the "*spell*" was lost. Dr. Witt, too, a sensible man, who owned and dwelt in the large house, since the Rev. Dr. Blair's, as well as old Mr. Frailey, who also acted as a physician, and was really pretty skilful, were both U——e doctors, (according to the superstition then so prevalent in Europe,) and were renowned also as conjurors. Then the cows and horses, and even children, got strange diseases; and if it baffled ordinary medicines, or Indian cures and herbs, it was not unusual to consult those persons for relief; and their prescriptions which healed them, as resulting from witchcraft, always gave relief! Dr. Frailey dwelt in a one-story house, very ancient, now standing in the school house lane. On each side of his house were lines of German poetry, painted in oil colours, (some of the marks are even visible now); those on one side have been recited to me, viz.:

Translated thus:

Lass Neider neiden,	Let the envious envy me,
Lass Hasser hassen;	Let the hater hate me;
Was Gott mir giebt	What God has given to me,
Muss mann mir lassen,	Must man leave to me.

An idea was very prevalent, especially near the Delaware and Schuylkill waters, that the pirates of Black Beard's day had deposited treasure in the earth. The fancy was, that sometimes they killed a prisoner and interred him with it, to make his ghost keep his vigils there and guard. Hence it was not rare to hear of persons having seen a *sphoke* or ghost, or of having dreamed of it a plurality of times, which became strong incentive to dig there. To procure the aid of a professor in the black art, was called *Hexing*; and Shrunk, in particular, had great fame therein. He affected to use a diviner's rod, (*a witch-hazel*) with a peculiar angle in it, which was supposed to be self-turned in the hands, when approached to any minerals; some use the same kind of rod now to *feel* for hidden waters so as to dig for wells. The late Col. T. F. used to amuse himself much with the credulity of the people. He pretended he could *hex* with a hazel rod; and often he had superstitious persons to come and offer him shares in spoils, which they had seen a *sphoke* upon! He even wrote and printed a curious old play to ridicule the thing.

CHAPTER VIII.

Charms and Superstitions.

Phebe Gibbons, in the book *"Pennsylvania Dutch," and Other Essays*, says:

Mrs. G., born in Lebanon county, says that when they were children one would take a looking-glass and go down the cellar-stairs backward, in order to see therein the form of a future spouse. Another custom was to melt lead and pour it into a cup of cold water, expecting to discover some token of the occupation of the same interesting individual. A person in York also remembers that at Halloween her nurse would melt lead and pour it through the handle of the kitchen door-key. The figures were studied and supposed to resemble soldier-caps, books, horses, and so on. This nurse was Irish, but the other domestics were German. A laboring woman from Cumberland county, and afterward from a "Dutch" settlement in Maryland, says that she has heard of persons melting lead to see what trade their man would be of. My German friend before quoted says that in the Palatinate they melted the lead on New-Year's eve. In Nadler's poems in the Palatinate dialect, St. Andreas' night is the time spoken of for melting the lead. This is the 30th of November. Further, in a work called "The Festival Year" (*Das Festliche Yahr*), by Von Reinsberg-Duringsfeld, Leipsic, 1863, the custom of pouring lead through the beard, or wards, of a key is mentioned.

A lawyer, born in Franklin county, tells me that it is a common superstition among Pennsylvania-Germans that persons born on Christmas night can see supernatural things and hear similar sounds. He adds that his mother told him of a person who was skeptical and ridiculed the idea, and was told to go out into his feeding-room and listen. He lay down on the hay, and while there one of the oxen said, *"Uebermorgen schieben mir unser Meschter auf den Kirchhof."* (Day after tomorrow we will haul our master to the graveyard.) And his funeral was on the day specified. My German friend before quoted says that in the Palatinate they believe that as it strikes twelve on Christmas eve, all animals talk together. She adds, "I think that idea is through Germany."

A gentleman connected with schools in Northampton county, says that at Halloween his daughters meet their companions and melt lead into water to tell their fortunes. They also fill their mouths with water that they may not speak, as speaking would break the charm; and walk around a block of houses. The first name which they hear is that of their future spouse. Another practice, which, unlike the foregoing, may be tried at any time of the year, is to take a large door-key and tie it within the leaves of a small Bible, the handle remaining out. Two girls rest the handle upon their fingers, and repeat some cabalistic verse; of which, he thinks, each line begins with a different letter, and the key will turn at the initials of the future spouse. These, he says, are the remnants of old superstitions, and he suspects that the human mind is naturally superstitious. He adds, "The population of Easton is mixed so that we cannot tell how many of these are purely German; but by going into the rural German districts of Northampton county you will find many strange ideas, such as that on a certain church festival, say Ascension day, you must not sweep your house, lest it become full of fleas."

A simple-minded woman in Lancaster county, who showed some regard for the Reformed Church, said that she had sat up late sewing the night before, so as not to sew on Ascension day. "My mother," she said, "knew a girl that sewed on Ascension day; and there came a gust and killed her."

One of my German acquaintances calls my attention to the salt-cake eaten in Lancaster. It is made extremely salt, and is eaten by girls, who then go to bed backward without speaking and without drinking; and he of whom they dream is to be their future husband. This, he says, is a custom also in Germany.

But the most universal ideas of this superstitious kind are those connected with the signs in the almanac. Baer's Almanac, published in Lancaster, still has the signs of the zodiac down the pages, like one shown to me in the Palatinate, where a man of some education said, "Here is where I see how to plant my garden." What, however, is very mysterious is that when our people tell us that you must not plant now, for IT is in the Posy-woman (and the things will all run to blossom, and not bear fruit), they cannot tell *what* is in the Posy-woman, or Virgo. I infer, however, that it is the moon.

I have been shown a German Bible, which belonged to the grandfather of one of my neighbors, wherein the family births were entered in the German language. I endeavored to decipher one, as follows:

"1797, *September den 9ten ist ein Sohn gebohren ihm Zeichen Witter, ehr ist ihn dem nehmlichen Mohnat ihm Herren entshlafen.*"

"On the 9th of September, 1797, a son is born to us in the sign of the Ram [Aries]. In the same month he fell asleep in the Lord."

The same neighbor who owns the Bible just mentioned tells me that one of the Russian Mennonites showed him a pamphlet in the German language, which the man had brought from Europe; wherein was told what would be the fortune of a child born in each sign, his health, wealth, etc.; but my neighbor says that he, himself, had no faith in it. "Grain should be sowed in the up-going; meat butchered in the down-going will shrink in the pot." But my worthy neighbors do not appear to know what it is that is going up and going down. I infer, of course, that it is the moon. Is it not remarkable that my neighbors should be so attached to book-farming? I knew a woman, born among Friends, but in a Pennsylvania-German settlement, who was lamenting the smallness of the piece of meat on the table. "What a little piece, and so big before it was cooked! How it has shrunk! It is in the down-going. And those straw-berries, too, that I preserved, that went away to so little; they were done in the down-going." But one of her family spoke up, bravely, "Just so, mother; that must be it. Now I know what's the matter with my portemonnaie, that it shrinks away so; it's the down-going."

These beliefs in the influence of the heavenly bodies must be the relics of astrology remaining in the almanacs, and never drawn now from actual observation of the weather and the planets.

Mrs. Nevin relates the following (Philadelphia *Press*, June 2, 1875): "There are several superstitions connected with death and funerals in the country, which are a strange blending of the ludicrous with the mournful. One is that if the mother of a family is dying, the vinegar-barrel must be shaken at the time to prevent the 'mother' in it from dying. Said a man once in sober earnest to me, 'I was so sorry Mr.

D. was not in the room when his wife died.' 'Where was he?'
'Oh, in the cellar a-shaking the vinegar-barrel; but if he
had just told me, I would have done it and let him been
in the room to see her take her last breath.'"

Mrs. Nevin adds: "Another superstition is that the last
person that goes out of a house at a funeral will be the next
one to die, and as the audience begins to thin, you may see
people slip very nimbly out of a back or kitchen door to
avoid being that last one."

The belief in *spooks* or ghosts is not lost in "Pennsylvania
Dutch" land. In some of his verses Mr. Schantz tells (Allentown *Friedensbote*) of an abandoned school-house standing near a sand-pit, beside some woods.

A Lutheran clergyman said lately, "I do not believe in
spooks myself, but plenty of people do; and sad enough it
is that there should be such superstition."

MEDICAL SUPERSTITIONS IN PENNSYLVANIA.

Gibbons' "*Pennsylvania Dutch*" book says:

The peculiarities of a people are always best observed by
those who do not live among them, or rather by those who
visit them occasionally. Most of my notes on this subject
are taken from the conversation of physicians born in other
localities than those in which they practice. One in my own
county mentions the "*apnehme*," (*obnema*), or wasting
away of children. He says that popular remedies are measuring the child and greasing it by certain old women. Another says that the "Pennsylvania Dutch" also measure for
wild-fire or erysipelas, generally using a red silk string, and
measuring about sundown. They blow across the affected
part to blow the fire outside of the string, at the same time
they "say words" or pow-wow. This physician says that the
greasing above mentioned is for liver-grown children, and
not for "abnehme" (as it is spelled). One class of pow-wow-
ers do not interfere, he says, with regular practitioners; but
one old woman in this county (who builds a fire in the brick
oven, and says words over the coals) has been known to hide
the prescriptions of regular physicians. He adds: "If a person is burned, recourse is sometimes had to a professional
blower, who blows across the surface, saying words in the
interval. Along the Pennsylvania Canal, on the Susquehanna,
where ague prevails, the patient who has a chill is tied to
a tree by a long string, and he runs around the tree until

the string is exhausted, and then on to some distance. This is tying the chill to a tree. A 'Pennsylvania Dutch' remedy for whooping-cough, and one by which they bother the millers a good deal, is to put the child into a hopper with grain, and let the child remain until the grain is all ground out. Blood-stopping is very common in Pennsylvania. I saw a man with an artery cut, in whose case a blood-stopper was called in. The man pressed his hand on the bleeding part and repeated something, raising his eyes to heaven; but the artery was too powerful for him."

On the west side of the Susquehanna the only county that can distinctively be called Pennsylvania-German is York. A physician in the borough says that town and county are full of superstitions. He says, "In case of hemorrhage from the nose, from a wound or from other cause, a common cure is to wrap a red woolen string round each finger; another is to lay an axe under the bed, edge upward; and you can't talk them out of it. I used to get angry when I first came here, but I found that it was of no use. These are not occasional things only, but I have seen them over and over again. Then there are prayers for stopping blood, always in 'Dutch.' They can't be sick in English, and the first question to me as a physician has been 'Kansht du Deutsch?' (Do you speak German?) One of the prayers for stopping blood is, I understand, for human beings, and another for animals; and I think that the names of the persons of the Trinity are introduced. I have often asked, but they are not allowed to tell. Soon after I came here, I ordered some boneset tea for a patient, and the mother asked in 'Dutch' whether the leaves should be pulled upwards or downwards. 'Will it make any difference?' I asked. 'Oh, yes; if you pull them upwards, it will work upwards; and if you pull them downwards, it will work downwards.' [A valuable hint for a physician if the same plant can be used both as an emetic and a purgative.] Of the blood of a black fowl,—no other color will do,—three drops are given internally. I think this is for convulsions; but I hear so many of these things, and have heard them so many years, that they make no impression on my mind. These are pure 'Pennsylvania Dutch' peculiarities; I have found none or few of them among foreign Germans."

I asked whether these ideas still continue or whether they are wearing out. "No," he said, "they don't wear out. I meet them every day. They will speak of horses and animals being bewitched (*verhext*). I have a story from good authority of a horse that was said to be *verhext*, and that turned out to have a nail in his hoof. That is a fact. What are you going to do about it?"

But to come to another county, Berks. I hear that in Reading there is a woman called the *Wurst-frau*, because her mother sold sausages and "puddings." This woman has a large office practice in salves and powwowing. In an adjoining county, Lehigh, I remember a few years ago to have seen the names of two persons put down in the directory as *powvowers;* the word being spelled as pronounced in 'Dutch.'

Norristown, in Montgomery county, is greatly Anglicized; but a physician says that an idea exists of stopping blood by a religious lingo, into which come the words *"der Vater, Sohn, und Heilig Geist."* "A certain man told me that he had never failed to arrest bleeding from wounds or even from the lungs, nor was it necessary to be upon the spot; he could go home and repeat his lingo. This was his only medical skill; he did not claim to be a doctor."

In Norristown also I met a woman who had been quite ill; but I heard that when better she would not get up on Sunday, lest she should never get well, and Friday was as bad. Her little grandchild having a birth-mark, she passed the hand of a dead person over it to take it away, but was unsuccessful.

```
A B R A C A D A B R A
  B R A C A D A B R
    R A C A D A B
      A C A D A
        C A D
          A
```
            —Magical Words.

CHAPTER IX.

DR. DADY AND THE "GHOSTS" OF YORK COUNTY IN 1797.

From Prof. I. Daniel Rupp's *History of Berks and Lebanon Counties,* we quote references to an account of Doctor Dady, an imposter, who tricked many people in Pennsylvania, before the 1800's. He first made an appearance at Millerstown, Lebanon county; then in Adams and York counties. We are reprinting it in full for the reason that it concerns Shrewsbury, York county, people, in close proximity to the place where Nelson D. Rehmeyer, 60, reputed "hex" doctor, met his death at the hands of Messrs. John H. Blymyer, 33, John Curry, 14, and Wilbert G. Hess, 18, (said to be "hexed" by Rehmeyer), on November 27, 1928.

The account is as follows:

It was at this place [Millerstown]—Rev. Dr. Dady—the noted impostor, first commenced, by aid of his fascinating eloquence, to gull the honest Germans. To show what may be done among a people believing implicitly—"men untried,"—that place is given to the following. A wholesome lesson may be deduced from it. When he failed, he tried another region, more genial to his purposes.

DOCTOR DADY.

The following account of that noted impostor, is taken nearly word for word from that written by the Hon. John Joseph Henry, and sent by him to Philadelphia with the convicted impostors. Judge Henry wrote the account from notes taken at the trial. It follows, in most things, the order of the testimony as given in by the witnesses.

Dr. Dady, who was a German by birth, came to this country with the Hessians during the American revolution. Possessing a fascinating eloquence in the German language, and being very fluent in the English, he was afterwards employed as a minister of the gospel by uninformed but honest Germans.

[56]

When the sacerdotal robe could no longer be subservient to his avaricious views, he laid it aside and assumed the character of a physician. As such he went to York county, and dwelt among poor inhabitants of a mountainous part thereof, (now within the limits of Adams county,) where, in various artful ways, he preyed on the purses of the unwary.

Of all the numerous impositions with which his name is connected, and to which he lent his aid, we will mention but two. The scene of one of them is in what is now Adams county, where he dwelt; and of the other in the "barrens" of York county.

The following is an account of the Adams county imposition:—

Rice Williams, or rather Rainsford Rogers, a New Englander, and John Hall, a New Yorker, (both of whom had been plundering the inhabitants of the southern states by their wiles,) came to the house of Clayton Chamberlin, a neighbor of Dady, in July, 1797.

On the following morning, Dady went to Chamberlain's, and had a private conversation between Williams and Hall, before breakfast. After Dady had left them, Williams asked Chamberlain whether the place was not haunted. Being answered in the negative, he said that it was haunted—that he had been born with a veil over his face—could see spirits, and had been conducted thither, sixty miles, by a spirit. Hall assented to the truth of this. In the evening of the same day, they had another interview with Dady. Williams then told Chamberlain, that if he would permit him to tarry over night, he would show him a spirit. This being agreed to, they went into a field in the evening, and Williams drew a circle on the ground, around which he directed Hall and Chamberlain to walk in silence. A terrible screech was soon heard proceeding from a *black* ghost (!!!) in the woods, at a little distance from the parties, in a direction opposite to the place where Williams stood. In a few minutes a *white* ghost appeared, which Williams addressed in a language which those who heard him could not understand — the ghost replied in *the same language!* After his ghostship had gone away, Williams said that the spirit knew of a treasure which it was permitted to discover to *eleven* men—they must be honest, religious and sensible, and neither horse jockeys nor Irishmen.

The intercourse between Williams and Dady now ceased to be apparent; but it was continued in private. Chamberlain, convinced of the existence of a ghost and a treasure, was easily induced to form a company, which was soon effected.

Each candidate was initiated by the receipt of a small sealed paper, containing a little yellow sand, which was called "the power." This "power" the candidate was to bury under the earth to the depth of one inch, for three days and three nights—performing several absurd ceremonies, too obscene to be described here.

A circle, two inches in diameter, was formed in the field, in the centre of which there was a hole six inches wide and as many deep. A captain, a lieutenant and three committee men were elected. Hall had the honor of the captaincy. The exercise was to take place around the circle, &c. This, it was said, propitiated and strengthened the white ghost, who was opposed by an unfriendly black ghost who rejoiced in the appellation of Pompey. In the course of their nocturnal exercises they often saw the white ghost—they saw Mr. Pompey, too, but he appeared to have "his back up," bellowed loudly, and threw stones at them.

On the night of the 18th of August, 1797, Williams undertook to get instructions from the white ghost. It was done in the following manner: He took a sheet of clean white paper, and folded it in the form of a letter, when each member breathed into it three times; this being repeated several times, and the paper laid over the hole in the centre of the circle, the instructions of the ghost were obtained. The following is a short extract from the epistle writen by the ghost:

"Go on, and do right, and prosper, and the treasure shall be yours. I am permitted to write this in the same hand I wrote in the flesh for your direction—O————☞☝. Take care of your powers in the fear of God our protector—if not, leave the work. There is a great treasure, 4000 pounds a-piece for you. Don't trust the black one. Obey orders.— Break the enchantment, which you will not do until you get an ounce of mineral dulcimer eliximer; some German doctor has it. *It is near, and dear, and scarce.* Let the committee get it—but don't let the Doctor know what you are about— he is wicked."

The above is but a small part of this precious communication. In consequence of these ghostly directions, a young man named Abraham Kephart waited, by order of the committee, on Dr. Dady. The Dr. preserved his *eliximer* in a bottle sealed with a large red seal, and buried in a heap of oats, and demanded fifteen dollars an ounce for it. Young

Kephart could not afford to give so much, but gave him thirty-six dollars and three bushels of oats for three ounces of it. Yost Liner, another of these wise committee men, gave the Doctor $121.00 for eleven ounces of the stuff.

The company was soon increased to 30 persons, many of whom were wealthy. Among those who were most miserably duped may be mentioned Clayton Chamberlain, Yost Liner, Thomas Bigham, William Bigham, Samuel Togert, John M'Kinney, James Agnew the elder, James M'Cleary, Robert Thompson, David Kissinger, George Sheckley, Peter Wikeart, and John Philips. All these and many other men were, in the words of the indictment, "cheated and defrauded by means of certain false tokens and pretences, to wit: by means of pretended spirits, certain circles, certain brown powder, and certain compositions called mineral dulcimer elixer, and Detericks' mineral elixer."

But the wiles of these imposters were soon exerted in other parts. The following is an account of their proceedings in and about Shrewsbury township, in York county. Williams intimated that he had received a call from a ghost resident in those parts, at the distance of forty miles from Dady's. Jacob Wister, one of the conspirators, was the agent of Williams on this occasion. He instituted a company of twenty-one persons, all of whom were, of course, most ignorant people. The same and even more absurd ceremonies were performed by these people, and the communications of the ghost were obtained in a still more ridiculous manner than before. The communications mentioned Dr. Dady as the person from whom they should obtain the dulcimer elixer, as likewise a kind of sand which the ghost called "Asiatic sand," and which was necessary in order to give efficacy to the "powers." Ulrich Neaff, a committee man of this company, paid Dr. Dady ninety dollars for seven and a half ounces of the elixer. The elixer was put into vials, and each person who had one of them, held it in his hand and shook it as he pranced round the circle; on certain occasions he annointed his head with it, and afterwards, by order of the spirit, the phial was buried in the ground.

Paul Baliter, another of the committee men, took with him to Dr. Dady's, a hundred dollars to purchase "Asiatic sand," at three dollars per ounce. Dady being absent, Williams procured from the Doctor's shop as much sand as the money would purchase. In this instance, Williams cheated the Doctor, for he kept the spoil to himself, and thence arose an overthrow of the good fraternity.

Each of them now set up for himself. Williams procured directions from *his* ghost, that each of the companies should despatch a committee to Lancaster to buy "Deterick's mineral elixer," of a physician in that place. In the meantime Williams and his wife went to Lancaster, where they prepared the elixer, which was nothing but a composition of copperas and cayenne pepper. Mrs. Williams, as the wife of John Huber, a German doctor, went to Dr. Rose, with a letter dated "13 miles from Newcastle, Delaware," which directed him how to sell the article, &c. The enormity of the price aroused the suspicion of Dr. Rose. In a few days the delegates from the committee arrived, and purchased elixer to the amount of $740.33. When the lady came for the money, she was arrested, and the secret became known. Her husband, Williams, escaped.

The Lancaster expedition having led to a discovery of the tricks of the imposters, a few days after the disclosures made by Mrs. Williams, an indictment was presented in the criminal court of York county, against Dr. John Dady, Rice Williams, Jesse Miller, Jacob Wister, the elder, and Jacob Wister, the younger, for a conspiracy to cheat and defraud. The trial took place in June following, and resulted in the conviction of Wister, the elder, and Dr. Dady—the former of whom was fined ten dallars, and imprisoned one month in the county jail, the latter fined ninety dollars, and sentenced to two years confinement in the penitentiary at Philadelphia.

Dady had just been convicted of participating in the conspiracy in Shrewsbury, when he and Hall were found guilty of a like crime in Adams county—whereupon Hall was fined one hundred dollars and sent to the penitentiary for two years, and Dady was fined one hundred and sixty dollars, and sentenced to undergo an additional servitude of two years in the penitentiary, to commence in June, 1880, when his first term would expire.

Thus ended the history of Doctor Dady, who certainly was not devoid of talent, who possessed a most winning address, and was a thorough master in quick and correct discernment of character. He reigned, for a season, with undisputed sway, in what was then the western part of York county. His cunning, for a long time, lulled suspicion to sleep. The history of his exorcisms should teach the credulous that the ghosts which appear now-a-days are as material as our own flesh.—*History of York County.*

CHAPTER X.

An Interview With a Pow-Wow Doctor.

Curious to learn some facts regarding pow-wowing, the author made diligent inquiry from one who, he understood, could heal. This man, in his 60's, is well preserved in body and mind, and freely answered all questions. It was surprising to have him answer so many queries in a way that bore out almost every theory that had already been set down on paper in preparation for this edition.

Without one's stenographer it is rather difficult to remember exactly what all has been said in an hour's conversation, but enough has been preserved from said visit to convince the writer that the one spoken to is a firm believer in pow-wowing. As said, for the most part, his answers, even those made to "leading questions," did not give much new material.

To start with, he descends from Pennsylvania-German stock, and had been taught to pow-wow by his mother. He could give no reason why one must teach the art to one of the opposite sex; said that he had never heard why; but that it was the unwritten rule, or custom.

This man declares that he never has used any drugs or recipes for any of the healings that he has undertaken. When asked whether he " tried " for any and all complaints, he said that he did not; that he took more interest in cases such as erysipelas (*wildfeiar*, for which he would " blow fire "), malnutrition (decay, or *obnema*; sometimes termed " rickets," a children's disease), and certain types of sore eyes. But he says that in years gone by he has stopped blood, by the recital of a well-known passage of Scripture, which at the moment he could not recall.

The writer has heard of numerous instances where this man had supposedly cured erysipelas.

For *obnema*, or malnutrition, a red silk thread must be provided by the parents, or from the home wherein the sick person is to be " tried for."

This " tried for," by the way, is described as the process of praying while attending a child, or with an adult. Babies, of course, are not able to respond in like manner as the healer directs for adults, but prayers are answered nevertheless in the same way as for adults. For children, it is presumed that the parents stand sponsor, as in all church affairs, and furthermore, it is said that a tender Father stands watch over these little ones, even more so than over those of mature years. Adults, however, most generally repeat the words, or prayer, of the healer, and in many cases, three times over.

Cures are not always effected in one trial. Sometimes the healer may try for half a dozen times, or even a dozen times, yet may not be successful. If not, they are usually obliged to give up, for faith may be lacking in the patient, or in the healer. But a genuine, well-prepared and learned-healer, with a receptive and a believing patient, quite frequently gets an answer, for complaints which are common to man.

Yes, there are " answers " to pow-wow efforts, just as much so as in the old time revival meetings when one could " feel religion coming on." The one feeling is just as plausible and probable as the other. If the healer has been successful in his effort he will almost surely get an answer, it is said. This is generally felt by a sudden chilly, creepy feeling, up and down the back of the healer. In minor cases probably this is not so much pronounced, but in more serious cases, and there are many, if much praying, or trying, is necessary, it is not improbable that the healer has some reaction. It may be reaction from the efforts, or an answer from " above," but the righteous some times do have and enjoy certain blessings that are denied others.

Pow-wowing, we have been told, should not be attempted by persons who have not reached the age of at least 30, or more years, nor by persons commonly called " profane." One must believe in God, and in the Holy Scriptures. None of weak or unsound bodies should " try " on, or for another person. Only those of strong constitutions should undertake to heal by this method. The reason set forth is that in the process of healing the natural strength seems to ebb away, as though to mutually assist and help the weaker body, and there are instances noted that where the second or third " trial " had so weakened other healers that they had to be placed in bed.

This informant could not tell when pow-wowing originated — except that it has been in practice for many years. He mentioned that a certain book was often used as an aid to pow-wow doctors. This he said was Hohman's *Long Lost Friend,* and the one he has at his home is similar to one in the possession of the author, and which was printed in Harrisburg, in 1856, and bound with wall-paper board covers.

He does not use the book, nor has he for years, for as explained, he had his " pet " cures, and preferred to assist any needy person when called on, at any time, or place.

When asked whether he wasn't afraid the medical profession (mentioned so frequently in the daily papers), might prosecute him if they found him " healing " people, he said that he could not see why they should. He said he never did, and never would accept anything for what he had done for others. But it has been the rule, he believes, that if any persons wanted to, of their own free will, give something to the healer, that there was nothing amiss in it; these pow-wow specialists are sometimes required to travel many miles to accommodate persons who request the treatment, and naturally some expense would be incident to such journey. His mother, he said, told him, " Don't you ever take anything from anyone if you ever do pow-wow for them." He said he thought it tended to destroy one's usual effectiveness.

Not long ago he joined the Episcopal church and he said that they have regular meetings there whereat prayers are offered for the " sick, lame and halt." One woman, deaf for many years, can now hear sounds and is being benefitted. The minister in charge, too, is being recognized, for someone recently threatened to institute proceedings against him, whether for healing or for attempting to heal without a professional medical certificate, we do not know. But the Episcopal Church is backing healing by faith and prayer, and many say " more power to her." If carrying a rabbit's left-hind-foot will bring good luck, or a horse-chestnut carried in a trouser's pocket ward off rheumatism, prayer and pow-wowing won't do any less, and in this the writer agrees with the pow-wow man.

He recounted one instance where a young man had a large blister on the lid of one of his eyes. This condition was causing the man much pain and inconvenience and medical aid seemed to do no good, as he said. So the pow-wow man asked the sufferer if he believed in pow-wowing. The other replied " You bet I do!" So they proceeded to a convenient place where they found a laborer who had about finished his noon meal and secured from him a plate, greasy from food, upon which the sign of the Cross (†) was made three times. This was held even with the patient's face not over a foot or so from his eyes. He was told to concentrate his gaze on the plate and repeat a prayer after the healer a certain number of times — probably three. This being done, nothing startling happened — until about twenty minutes later, when the blister burst! and gave the patient immediate relief, and the start of an early cure.

Why he used the plate he could not fully explain, except that he knew his mother to have treated a similar case in that manner many years before, and in one " try " only, he received his answer. The recipe for this cure is noted in Hohman's *Long Lost Friend*.

The pow-wow man above referred to, is a prominent Harrisburg man, whose name, if mentioned, would bring many an answer, " Why, I know him."

CHAPTER XI.

Occasional Confidential Talks With Skeptics, et al.

The author has, perhaps, an unusual advantage over the average person who makes no special effort to secure data on the beliefs and superstitions of mankind, especially with reference to Pennsylvanians. A daily contact with people in almost all walks of life certainly develops some strange and enlightening conversations and situations.

The manner of approach to strangers is difficult quite often, and what might prove most interesting developments, must pass by. But there are others who will talk, and talk freely on almost any subject. Today, January 3, 1929, for instance, one, an almost daily caller, when shown a copy of the *Long Lost Friend* for the purpose of " drawing him out," threw up his hands in horror. This person objected to any and all parts of the pow-wow art, on general principles, and without knowing any of its material parts. He condemns the person who goes about in the practice of such art, or who stays at home for that matter, and attacks a certain church denomination for its practices of healing, more especially because the now deceased head of the church is placed on such an unusually high spiritual plane — even on a par with the Master, it is claimed. We suggested that each class, or group of people, had a right to pray, or heal, as they saw fit, since it was apparent that the world was too large and varied in its tastes, to be satisfied with one or two church denominations! He said that he'd like to talk that matter over for about three or four hours, which he did not, however, through lack of time. This man's mind is " fixed," and he is determined that a Christian can pray and get good results, but if he has to pow-wow, or act in a supposedly mysterious way —" nothing doing," as he said. His attitude is like those who believe that they can cast spells, or perform other spectacular phenomena — but which is neither more nor less than natural, and not produced by supernatural conditions, at all. His mind, like those who believe they can cast spells, in the everyday language of the street, is called a " single track " mind.

Another opinion we narrate as having followed closely after the above conversation.

A woman of mature years, about 52, said " Do you sell ' dream books '? You know it may seem strange to you, and I am not at all superstitious; but I like to look at dream books, and study them. So many, many, of my dreams come true, and I think I will want a book about dreams. I'm not superstitious," she repeated, " but I believe in dreams. My former pastor, the Rev. Dr. H——, used to say to me, ' don't keep your dreams too far from you.' I'll take this dream book, it looks pretty good!" This woman was asked whether she believed in pow-wowing. " Oh, my, no! Isn't it just awful how things are mixed up down in Lancaster and York counties?"

If only the reader could follow the various experiences of a book dealer from day to day! The publication of the various conditions of mankind, their beliefs, their superstitions, their down-right ignorance in many cases, (based on the kinds of books they read, and from what they tell unconsciously in the course of conversation, all of which the dealer can draw from many of those with whom he comes in contact), would make more than interesting reading — it would form a very considerable contribution to the folk-lore and custom literature of the age.

In the foregoing the man believed prayer by a Christian would effect good; but by the pow-wow method, no matter how good the man or woman might be, no matter how sincere the effort — he would not believe in its having a place in everyday life. To differentiate between the two methods would require much time and talent!

The woman mentioned, prominent in a local church, is not at all superstitious (she says), but believes in dreams. Yet dreams, the common affairs of the night, are said to be caused by a condition of the body — indigestion, congestion, slight strictures, etc., which pass in a flash of time, and which are recalled in the morning; dreams are also sometimes fostered by an easily pliable mind, and what we sometimes say about the " wish being father to the thought " may be applied with reason to what many persons have believed to be " dreams " revealing great prophecies, etc.

On December 19, 1928, one Charles D. Lewis, colored, observed that he had carried a *Pow-Wow* book with him at all times for a period of 16 years, and had never, in that length of time, had an accident. (The author of the *Pow-Wow* book claims that the person who carries said book with him will thus be protected, and from which assertion many persons have, in years gone by, followed the suggestion, and claim to have been immune from many of the pitfalls in life). He lost his book just a short time previous to the above date, and seems to have had his first accident after its loss. He was happy, he said, to have procured another copy. He claims to have been a much-traveled man, too, having been a fireman for several large steamship companies, whose ships carried him into almost all waters of the world. He was on board a White Star liner during the late World War, as a fireman, and while in the vicinity of Suez, his ship was taken over, and assigned to the British Admiralty Service, and said Lewis was mustered into the British navy. He thereby became what was likely the only Harrisburg man to serve in His Majesty's navy during the war. In his many miles of travel he claims that possession of the book preserved him against accidents. He seems to carry it for that reason, and not that he ever makes use of it as a pow-wow "doctor."

CHAPTER XII.

An Amulet Used During the World War.

During the late World War, while the author was engaged in the publishing of a newspaper, following closely after the declaration of war by the United States, and previous to his own enlistment, he received an order from some person in a nearby village for a small job of printing. At that time no particular attention or notice was paid to it, although "samples" of it, like all commercial printing jobs, were faithfully kept over a series of years.

Upon the opening up of the discussion of pow-wowing and the like, we recalled the "Letter of Protection," which we had been engaged to print more than 10 years ago.

The number printed at that time was not large,—say one or two hundred. These, we understood at the time, were to be distributed by the party who purchased them, to young men who entered the army from Snyder, Union, Juniata and Mifflin counties, friends of the donors, and from our knowledge and experience with these people in a life-time residence among them, we feel sure that nearly every lad who was fortunate enough to be presented with a copy of the "Letter," carried it with him during the whole period of his enlistment. Experience teaches that it pays to be superstitious during war times, especially while in the service.

There's just a little bit of satisfaction, during such seasons as wars, it seems, to have some assurance, however "foolish" it might seem at any other time, and doubtless many a lad placed much, or at least a small faith in the letter. A copy of it, still preserved, will bear reprinting at this time as a record of the folk-lore and beliefs at this late date.

The letter reads as follows:

A Letter for Protection.

In the name of God the Father, the Son and Holy Ghost: As Christ stopped at the Mount of Olives, all guns shall stop. Whoever carries this letter with him he shall not be damaged through the enemy's guns or weapons, God will give him strength; he may not fear robbers and murders, nor guns, pistols, swords and muskets shall not hurt him through the command of the Angel Michael, in the name of the Father, Son and the Holy Ghost, God with me. Whoever carries this letter with him he shall be protected from all danger and he who does not believe in it may copy it and tie it to the neck of a dog and shoot at him and he will see that it is true. Whoever has this letter shall not be taken prisoner, nor wounded by the enemy. Amen. As true as it is that Jesus Christ died and ascended to Heaven and suffered on earth he shall not be shot, but shall stand unhurt, and adjure all guns and weapons on earth by the living God, the Father, the Son and the Holy Ghost, I pray in the name of Christ's blood that no ball shall hit me, be it gold or silver, but that God in Heaven may deliver me of all sins in the name of the Father, the Son and Holy Ghost. This letter fell from Heaven and was found in Holstine in 1724. It was written in golden letters and moved over the baptism of Madaginery, and when they tried to seize it, it disappeared until 1791, that everybody may copy and communicate it to the world. There was further written in it whosoever works on Sunday he shall be condemned. You shall not work on Sunday but go to church and give the poor of your wealth; for you shall listen to the word of God. If you do not I will punish you with hard times, epidemics and war. I command you that you shall not work too late on Saturday. Be you rich or poor you shall pray for your sins that they may be forgiven. Do not swear by His name. Do not desire gold or silver. Do not fear the intrigues of men; sure as fast as I create you so fast I can crush you. Also, be not false with your tongue; respect father and mother; do not bear false testimony against your neighbors, and I will give you health and peace. But he who does not do so, or does not believe in this, shall be left by me and shall not have happiness or blessing. If you do not convert yourself you certainly will be punished at the day of judgement for what you cannot account for your sins. Whoever has this letter in his house lightning shall not strike it. All women who carry this with them shall bring forth living fruit. Keep my commandments which I sent to you through my angel. In the name of Jesus. Amen.

CHAPTER XIII.

An Account of Pow-Wowing by a Correspondent.

The Lancaster *News and Intelligencer-Journal*, for Sunday, December 23, 1928, contains an interesting account on Pow-Wowing, by our friend Mr. H. K. Landis, who, with his brother George D. Landis, are proprietors of one of the best equipped and largest private museums, in any rural section of the country. These men are students of history, and folk-lore, the former especially being an authority on bibliography, maps, old glass, iron (hand-wrought), old farming implements, tools, milling equipment, household effects of all kinds, etc.

Mr. Landis, when interviewed by the newspaper reporter, gave quite an interesting account from his general knowledge of the custom. Research in his extremely interesting, and valuable library on Americana, Ethnology and Folk-Lore, would bring out much additional matter, we have no doubt.

The reporter for the Lancaster paper says:

Deadly feuds among highjackers are so frequent as to be classed among the common occurences, but the recent fatal conflict of pow-wow practitioners stirred up so much interest that the state authorities themselves propose to investigate. It is surprising that the practice of so-called sorcery should be backed by such general credulity. Even those who cry out most loudly their disbelief are among the foremost to exclaim: "Don't you dast put a spell on me!" One seldom thinks of these things until something happens and then follows surprise at such a possibility. So, when we dropped into the shop of the Landis Valley Museum, north of Lancaster, we accosted the bookish brother with: "What do you know about pow-wowing; is there such a thing?"

"No doubt about it," he replied. "All through historic time the practice of magic and sorcery was strongly evident. Many were the ways in which it was manifested, and the pow-wow practices are but a mild survival. Its origin is about two-thirds German, but England also retains many of these credulities. The later American additions are ridiculous and nonsensical in comparison with the "remedies" which preceded. In the minds of the people, the belief in signs, talismans, old saws, sayings formed on Scriptural quotations, "haus segen," "himmelsbriefe," books like the "Lang Verborgene Freund,"—all these are believed in (sometimes half-heartedly with the reservation, "Well, it can do no harm") and put in practice. There are very many of these sayings. Fogel collected over two thousand of them. However ridiculous and irrational, they are readily accepted when introduced with: "They say." When one meets a fact one does not say "pooh-pooh," and it is a fact that a large percentage of our people are not antagonistic to the superstitions handed down from their parents and forefathers, nor are they entirely disbelievers. Of course, there is nothing in these mystical rites, outside of the purely psychological effect of faith, although that is a factor to be reckoned with, but they are an interesting study in social customs."

"My grandmother had a cow which had lain for days unable to rise. She informed a visiting lady about it and was told "She is bewitched—let me see her." Entering the stable she repeated "Yah, Sie ist verhext." Making some signs in the air, on the stable door jamb, and mumbling some words, she left. The next day the cow was at the trough as usual. My grandmother shook her head and said that now she did not know what to think. A book could be filled with such narratives, told in all sincerity. Of course, there is a natural explanation, but when the story teller wants to think it was supernatural, there is no changing his mind. So, these stories persist.

"There are many groups of these superstitions and sayings, the most important of which are remedies for ailments for man and beast, omens and luck, children, planting and crops, weather and zodiac signs, dreams, etc. Probably the more harmful are those where charms and soothsaying replaces the physician. For example, to cure convulsions in a child, place under its pillow a worn horseshoe having all the nails in it; or, cover the child with its father's wedding coat; if it eats the first hailstone seen after its birth, it will have no convulsions; to cure them, salt put into the hands and onions tied to the feet of the sufferer also are advised. No wonder so many children died!

"Whooping cough" is another serious disorder. Wear the

rattles of a rattle-snake to cure it, they say. Baptismal water
is beneficial; also a drink of stolen milk; wearing a piece of
stolen blue ribbon helps; for the patient to kiss a negro child
is a remedy. One is advised to cut up and feed to the child
the cast off skin of a snake; or, we can put a spider in a
bag to be hung about the child's neck; putting a trout's
mouth into that of the child, is directed by several. When
the nose bleeds, let three drops fall upon a stone picked up and
replace it as found, when the bleeding ceases. Picking up a
stone, spitting upon it, and replacing as found has much
merit; it prevents cramp while swimming, stops stitches in
the side, etc.

"To cure a child from "obnema" or "the waste," feed it
with a stolen spoon. To avoid having a headache, put on
your right stocking first. Erysipelas, or wild fire, is often
treated by pow-wowing; or, sparks from steel striking flint
are made to fall upon the affected places. To ward off convulsions and sickness from children, dig up burdock roots
of first year growth, cut into three pieces, thread them and
wear as a necklace; again, for convulsions, wear a necklace
of beads turned from the root of the peony. These are but
a few of the sayings and curious practices as used by people
themselves.

"The pow-wow or practitioner goes a step further sometimes, by posing as exercising supernatural powers, colored
here and there by magic, sorcery, personality, testimonials and
the force of cumulative belief throughout his community.
The "hexa-buch" to which he appears to refer is closely
guarded as of great secrecy and value, which it is not, as these
books are published in frequent and large editions available
to any one. Hohman's "Long Lost Friend" can be bought
in almost any large book store at one dollar per copy. The
field covered in this practice includes the laying of spells,
witching, removing spells, and quite the most frequently,
the accepting of liberal fees. No education is required, no
diploma or certificate is obtained; the doctor may be male
or female, black or white, yet deluded souls flock to them
for advice, comfort, cures or perhaps vengeance. A veil of
secrecy surrounds these seances. The wonder is not that they
exist, but rather that they are under neither restriction nor
inspection. Maybe even the officials of the state are nervous
over an invisible hand stretching out toward them out of
the darkness. But, let us drop that for the present as I want
to talk to you about the framed benedictions on the walls

of the credulous. Here is one, decorated with birds, angels and fruit and containing several verses, with this heading:

HAUS-SEGEN

In den drey allerhochsten Namen,
Vater, Sohn and Heil'ger Geist,
Dies das chor der Engel priesst
Gesundheit, Ru' und Segen, amen.

It blesses the home and land, the crops, cattle and protects against fire and accident, hail and lightning, frost and hopes that the family live happily and prosper.

Another example is entirely pen work, illuminated and well preserved, written in German script, the last line stating that it belonged to William Schumacher, a distiller; it is dated 1826, and begins thus:

Jesu, wohn in meinem Haus
Weiche nimmermehr daraus

He asks the Lord to remain in his home and never again leave it or he would be desolate and continues: Oh you great giver of blessings, come and bestow upon us joy, fortune and health; just as Job and Abraham received rich blessings so do with me. And so on to the signature.

Again, we find on the walls, framed and colored, illustrations, representations of the Lord's Prayer; mottoes such as "God Bless Our Home;" the baptismal covenant with illustrations; Adam and Eve in wood cut illustrations with the story of the fall in verse. Occasionally one sees a gilded horse shoe; in the Bible will be found a dried four-leafed clover, pressed flowers, or a lock of hair; men carry "lucky" pocket pieces, children wear amulets and the women know all the signs. Many other curious things are found in the museum.

CHAPTER XIV.

A Few Illustrative Accounts.

We have taken just a few moments to write several accounts under different "headings" — all of which are more or less related to the subject — pow-wowing, or natural phenomena—or coincidence. Many others might be brought together, as might testimonials by persons who would personally claim to have received benefits direct from pow-powing. Just how these benefits were brought about, would, most generally, be attributed to a natural sequence.

Psychology, healing naturally in course of time, faith, etc., all enter into and come under one main head which would vary to suit the tastes of the critic.

The following are a few of various types which we might classify under "magic," or "witchcraft" or superstition.

A MIRACLE.

The item to which we shall make reference, appeared in the Lancaster *New Era*, January 8, 1929. We haven't read that issue of the paper, but the story was sent to us and the sum and substance of it is this: "Says Hex Book Saved His Life." The first son of a seventh daughter carried the *Long Lost Friend* and the *Psalms* in the pocket of his automobile. While out on the road it appears that the driver, Warren H. Weber, 22, met with an accident; his machine having been struck by a locomotive. Weber said later: "When the train struck us I immediately thought of my books, and then felt safe." How badly used the machine was, we do not know, but the newspaper seems to indicate that Weber lived, and that his confidence was in his books. Was this a modern-day miracle?

AN AMULET.

This story is probably every bit as credible as any other of its kind circulated during the past generation, when persons carried amulets to protect them from bullets, drowning, bodily injury, and the like. Since the greatly increased use

of the automobile it has been called to the author's attention
that men and women belonging to a well-known Church,
have been encouraged to believe that the attaching of "stick-
ers" and printed cards of a certain specified kind, in their
automobiles at all times, protects said automobile from the
probabilities of accident! We don't refer to any insurance
policy, either. We have seen countless instances of persons
carrying these amulets, or letters of protection, on their
persons, in card cases, or charms about their necks attached
to chains or cords, but the use of a "new series" of charms
for one's automobile is new to the most of us, doubtless.
It requires a great deal of "faith" these days, in amulets,
and everything else, to ward off accidents and troubles to
our automobiles.

Some persons are addicted to the habit of smoking a certain
brand of cigarets, because the wrapper on such packages has
a kind of type for advertising the "brand" that has a cross
(†), or what appears to be such, wherever the letter "t"
ought to occur. Are smokers of this brand superstitious?

INCONSISTENCY.

There are any number of persons who have a dread and
fear of used, or shall we say second-hand, books. Second-
hand books are those which are usually obtained by a book
dealer from persons who have purchased them new, and who
are about to move, or clean house; or from the estates of
persons who have passed away. These books, figuratively,
have been in but one family since purchased new. Then they
come to the dealer. So many people wouldn't buy a second-
hand book because of their belief that such books contain
"germs!" Yet it may be said that times without number,
these same people will go to their public, or lending libraries, and borrow books that have been in dozens and dozens
of hands, out in all kinds of weather, and places; time and
again in the hands of those who were sick, and with illnesses
that might shock the modest person. These same persons who
are afraid of book germs, handle Uncle Sam's money, (because that is the only worth-while coin in this country),
and if anything can, and does carry more "germs" than the
common medium of exchange, it certainly must be something
unusually filthy! This is a typical picture of persons who
fear, or dread, or are suspicious as well as superstitious in
common affairs of the day. They are inconsistent.

A STRANGE CURE.

Here's a barber shop story, told by a man whose salary runs about a thousand *a month*, and who ought to know what he's talking about, if no one else does. The story is laid in Pottstown. A mill official there claims that his wife has tried all the leading, and other physicians in that city, for relief from what appeared to be a blistered condition to her feet and lower limbs, which these physicians claimed came from diabetic troubles, and that they had been doing all they could for her relief, but that they doubted whether she could ever be cured. Undaunted, the husband, hearing of a pow-wow doctor living in the vicinity of Boyertown, traveled thence with his wife in search of the "faith healer." The latter was found, and—the point we wish to make plain to the reader is: The woman has entirely recovered, and is apparently as well as ever! Was this a Strange Cure?

A SHAMEFUL IMPOSITION!

This instance, we understand, has been investigated by officials of the State of Pennsylvania, although we do not have it *direct*. We doubt whether it could be obtained direct, on account of the officials feeling that they were giving something away. They did, unconsciously, it is said; and here it is: A certain man in Steelton, which adjoins the city of Harrisburg, went to a so-called pow-wow doctor in his home town. He went there feeling very much dejected, and run down. The "pow-wow" man's advice was sought. This is what he was told to do, according to accounts available: He was to have nightly ———— with his wife, week after week, until the "pow-wow doctor" should order otherwise, under penalty of certain conditions made at the time. But nature stepped in, and the wife complained of her inhuman treatment to a justice of the peace, who ruled that he had no jurisdiction in the matter, but that she should complain to the State Department, which we understand she did, and thus the story gained credence. The health of both the man and woman, was about ruined, which caused the latter to seek some form of relief. For a "pow-wow doctor" to suggest any such "cure" is most reprehensible, to say the least. And his fee was $5.00, or more. What a Shameful, Disgraceful Imposition!

A COINCIDENCE.

Some years ago a young man was engaged in doing some bark peeling, in the woods near a village in Snyder county. He was busy on a particularly nice piece of timber, and was doing remarkably well with it, when his attention was attracted to a hole which had been bored into the tree, not far from the butt. In this hole, about an inch in diameter, he found a lock of black hair, apparently belonging at one time to a human being. This startled him, and calling to an older man nearby, asked him what he could make out of the situation. He replied that it was nothing out of the ordinary. That some time before that, a young lad in the village had been for a number of years a sufferer of falling-fits. Medical aid had been sought, and all recommendations tried, but nothing seemed to give the youngster the desired relief. One day an old woman came to the house on a visit, and while there, the youngster had one of his fits. She inquired whether the parents had tried to stop the affliction, and they said they had, but nothing seemed to help. Whereupon she offered, if they didn't care, to pow-wow, assuring them that it would stop then. The parents were loath to submit, but eventually they agreed, and the placing of the hair in this particular tree was a part of the plan for relief. Relief,—rather cure,—for from the day the woman called there has never been a repetition of the fits. The young man grew into manhood, and has for years been a successful principal in the schools of a prominent Pennsylvania city. Was it a coincidence that the fits should cease with the placing of the hair in the tree, and the saying of a few words? Figure it out for yourself.

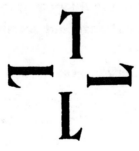

CHAPTER XV.

A Pointed Word to Those Who Scoff — Read It!

In summarizing, let it be said and understood, that the theories and accounts advanced in this treatise, have been obtained from most reliable and trust-worthy sources; from personal contacts and observations in a life-time residence with the people about whom we have essayed to speak. That superstition and belief in witchcraft, etc., should exist in this day and age, to some persons may seem incredible. Of course, what has been said about the subject proves beyond the shadow of a doubt that it is present more or less in force and practice. Just how serious it may be, or seem to be, may be based almost entirely on the doubter's, or believer's point of view. If, and when, a conspired attempt, on the part of several persons, under the term of magic, witchcraft, or any other similar name, to subvert or subject the will of another, or others, to do certain biddings, or to believe in certain forecasts or prophecies, spells and the like, is present *in force*, a serious menace to social life might be said to exist. Until then there should be little cause for alarm, for we are slowly recovering from the effects of a condition that had its inception ages and ages ago, and which will heal of itself, if left alone. The isolated case, of a mentally deranged man accidentally killing another whose mental condition is also said to have been " queer," should not upset the equilibrium of a State and Nation as rational and sensible as ours is said to be. Shame!

The State *cannot drive out superstition*, as one would *blow out a match!* Yet we have any number of persons, wise and otherwise, who think they are smart enough to do so. "Let him who is without sin, cast the first stone." In this matter of superstition, the person who seeks to *drive it out by force*, is but "one mule calling another mule, a *mule."* When you attempt to *drive* out superstition, you run great chances of closing, or seriously implicating all your places of religious worship! The intelligent person knows this; so for the sake of those who are good church members now, the less said of it the better. Remember a saying of years ago: "You can drive a horse to water, but you can't make him drink."

We are reminded of the simple little ditty concerning "Little Bo Peep." If these superstitious people are at all worth-while "salvaging", let us place as much confidence in them as did "Little Bo Peep." They are as precious and worth-while to the rest of mankind, as the sheep was to Bo Peep.

Let them alone, and they'll come home,
Dragging their tails behind them.

Let any man, be he Protestant, Catholic, Jew or Mohammedan, or what ever, conscientiously say that there are no "hidden meanings," no so-called "miracles," no "mystical rites," no *superstitions*, if you please, in their church-life somewhere, if not plentiously.

What church or sect does not foist some form or other, of it upon its believers? What church or sect is therefore not greatly benefitted by the imposition that they practice on their members, and which the members seem to have the greatest soul-delight in?

Why pick on the so-called ignorant Pennsylvania-Germans, or whoever it may be, when millions and millions dip their hands in "holy water," and make the sign of the cross dozens of times daily — why? — to purify and sanctify themselves; and to ward off evil, because they are superstitious.

Even the intelligent man or woman who does not believe in, or unconsciously practice some form of religious expression, or superstition under any other name, has yet to be born!

For the want of knowledge as to the meaning of certain acts one does in the course of a day, or a year, we often give it a name; however unrelated the name may be to the act.

Thus pow-wowing, casting of spells, prophecies, divination, mental telepathy, fortune-telling, crystal-gazing, and pure guess-work, are among many which are indiscriminately gathered under the terms of witchcraft, black magic, or pow-wowing.

One authority says " The Hebrew word *mekaseepah* literally means one who makes spells, amulets, poisons, and incantations, and corresponds to the Latin *venefica*. It is probable therefore that the name " witch " mentioned in the Bible had a different meaning to that applied to it in later times." In this connection it might be interesting to the reader to learn what Sir Walter Scott has to say:

" Witches were generally old, blear-eyed, wrinkled dames, ugly and crippled, frequently papists, and sometimes atheists; of cross-grained tempers and cynical dispositions. They were often poisoners and generally mono-maniacs. Epilepsy and all diseases not understood by the physicians were set down to the influence of witches. They were said to make two covenants with the devil, one public and one private. Then the novices were presented to the devil in person, and instructed to renounce the Christian faith, tread on the Cross, break the fasts, joining hands with Satan, paying him homage and yielding him body and soul. Some witches sold themselves for a term of years, and some for ever; then they kissed the devil, and signed their bond with blood, and a banquet ended the meeting, their dances being accompanied with shouts of ' Ha, ha! Devil, devil! Dance here, dance here. Play here, play here! Sabbath, sabbath!' Before they departed, the devil was said to give them philtres and amulets."

The ever increasing number of words in the English language, and the inability on the part of more than a small percentage of people to know all, or just a small number of these words, and what word to use at the right time, has caused much of the annoyance and mistaken ideas present today. One word may mean many different things; likewise one thing may have many different words. So the average person is taxed to more than he can bear, or acquire, and consequently is compelled to use the English, not as "she should be wrote or spoken," but as "she is convenient to the masses."

In this way the art of healing, which is no more mystifying than prayer! has been looked upon by various people as being nefarious, or sinful, and with its synonymous term of "pow-wow," (which really is in the vernacular), it has been brought under the very distasteful term of witchcraft, and black art, and magic.

If as much sin and spell-casting is being done today in the name of the devil as is generally attributed to what is called "voodooism," and the like, woe be to those who expect to be recipients of a rosy after-life. Hell would be a promising place for much of man-kind, under such beliefs and imaginations. And since so much criticism and ridicule has been directed toward the Pennsylvania-Germans especially, who as a whole are a peaceful, industrious, law-abiding class of citizens, we must relate a story told some years ago about these home-loving, Christian people; whatever else may be said about them and their superstitions.

The story is entitled "A Pointer to People Who Ridicule the Pennsylvania-Germans." It is attributed to ex-Senator Evan Holben. "A bevy of jack-a-dandies with fuzzy-wuzzy faces and summer girls with their dresses cut off above, sojourned a few days where the inhabitants were all very highly proficient in the Pennsylvania-German tongue. They liked the cooking, they relished the victuals, they enjoyed the invigorating atmosphere. In fact, they could stomach all except the language, which they hated. 'Too much Dutch here, there and everywhere,' was the common voice. Finally they packed up and went to the depot, where they heard some more Dutch; 'too much Dutch,' heard from every one. After they had been snugly seated in the car, two men with dinner pails came in talking Pennsylvania-German. 'Too much Dutch,' was the chorus of the coterie. One of the men said: 'My young friends, when you go away from home again, you GO TO HELL, *WHERE YOU WON'T HEAR ANY DUTCH.'*"

We are told that a person whose hearing is normal can *hear* the noise caused by a nearby explosion, but that of the explosion itself there is no noise — except that which is registered on that little sounding board in the individual's ear. This you see requires presence of man with his normal hearing faculty to produce a circuit, or to make the *sound* an actual fact, or reality.

In the matter of superstition, a rule may be applied that will fit any person — " as a man thinketh in his heart [and mind] so is he;" either good, bad, or indifferent. Witchcraft and superstition may be wide-spread, but its influences we believe to be negligible because of the mildness of their possible application. That witchcraft and spell-casting is very efficacious, we doubt, for the reason that with even as much general ignorance as is prevalent, not enough minds are so utterly blank or shallow as to fall willing slaves to the evil designs and works of those who would seek to work such charms.

Even though strange beliefs may extend over a great part of Pennsylvania, their importance to every day life and affairs is negligible and practically unfelt, since it appears that many years have elapsed since any " serious " cases have come to the attention of any of the courts in the Commonwealth.

CHAPTER XVI.

Overcoming Superstition — Conclusion.

How can we overcome superstition and disbelief in "far away" things which have no being, when every child, from the moment of its birth is rocked to sleep with

Rock-a-bye Baby, in the tree top, etc.?

When children can first understand, and comprehend their parent tongue, what are they told? They are told about the fairies, the goblins, Santa Claus, the Easter "bunny" that *lays eggs* (a German invention now in practice in many countries), the "boog-a-boo" man, etc. Children are told all these things, and more. Your book shelves are testimony as to that fact.

Now are there actually fairies, goblins, and the like? If not, then all superstition should be driven from the human race, in course of time. But if there are no fairies, no goblins, no "Little Red Riding-Hood," no "Three Bears," then no one has a moral right to teach the growing mind of a child anything but the truth! The present home-life of peoples in all nations, civilized and uncivilized, is "fairy" stories and therefore myths, or "false truths," (superstition), from the cradle to the grave!

The men who complain the loudest and longest and cry out against pow-wowing — superstition — or whatever it is, would be quite antagonistic against anyone who by law, or otherwise, should attempt to deprive them of the right to think as *they* pleased! to deprive them of the right to teach *their* children as they please — be it ever so insignificant a story as the "Three Bears," all decked out in "bib and tucker!"

If superstition is bad in the poor and others who practice pow-wowing, then its bad in the rest of us, in other forms of belief and practice — and we cannot *elect* to go *where* we will, but we'll all go down to Hell together!

If the men who presume to mould "public opinion" examine themselves first, and then go into the phase of *how* superstition can be wiped out in their neighbor's lives, as well as their own, they will find themselves thoroughly enmeshed in the tentacles of a "devil-fish."

The entire educational system in the beginner's life is based on myth. Mythology has been the gospel for unnumbered millions for ages. Change it? Try it!

The human race is not infallible, hence we have those who profess leadership, but who lack the necessary qualifications whereby others can follow in truth. If we are to emulate the Christ, then we have the Christian's example of what we ought to be like. But we cannot fully attain perfection, and it is for each of us to examine ourselves diligently, and correct our own wrong-doings. Be careful that in the attempt to bring about a new era in the history of the world by the elimination of "witchcraft," that we do not lose that which has already been hard to gain and retain, and which is all-precious to us!

Remember past history; our ancestors; our parents; the length of time it has taken to reach the state of learning that we now have.

The writer is not at all socialistic, or revolutionary in thought, but it might be suggested in passing, that if the poor, and ignorant (who are said to be so confoundedly superstitious), would be permitted to marry into the homes and families of those who have reached the "acme of perfection," we might be able to curb ignorance and superstition somewhat. Perish that thought! Public educators, and others, who have stirred up the witchcraft matter these past two months; legislators who would seek by law to limit a man as to what they want him to know, and still others, might make the first step, or sacrifice, in offering flesh of their flesh, and blood of their blood, to the most flagrant cases to come to their attention; and if witchcraft and superstition is to be stopped we know of no better plan than that to start with.

Other plans, like remolding our Church and School systems, would follow in due course, as our new generation of "sanctified" and holy angels began to make their appearance.

In conclusion:—We trust that the reader has had a full and satisfactory opportunity to study the subject of which we have just touched the surface. The presence of superstition, yes, even pow-wowing or witchcraft, in mild form, is not denied. To make a serious attempt to *drive* it out spontaneously, we fear, would cause a serious back-fire.

All in all, since the whole world is involved in its practice and belief in one form or another, we doubt whether any one would want to seriously undertake to "angelize" the people of one State, let alone the Nation, or the World!

We already have a great deal of wisdom, and are learning more from day to day. The much talked-of Heathen Chinese have a proverb that "One learns something every time a book is opened!" Those who are superstitious, and who believe in witches may do so; it will be hard to change their minds. Those who are ever so learned and wise, we refer to the counsel of Horace, to

Mingle a little folly with thy wisdom.

AN ACCOUNT OF

THE

"Witch" Murder Trial

YORK, PA.,

JANUARY 7-9, 1929.

COMMONWEALTH OF PENNSYLVANIA

vs.

JOHN BLYMYER, *et al.*

———

By A. Monroe Aurand, Jr.

*Former Newspaperman, and Author of Various Books on
Pennsylvania History, Folk-Lore and Biography.*

———

Privately Printed by
THE AURAND PRESS
HARRISBURG, PA.

1929

THE "WITCH" MURDER TRIAL AT YORK

"How do you find the defendant, guilty, or not guilty?"

"Guilty!"

"In what degree?"

"Guilty of murder in the first degree, with the recommendation of life imprisonment!"

Thus did the jury in the case of the Commonwealth of Pennsylvania vs. John H. Blymyer, in York county, find the defendant, on the charge of the murder of Nelson D. Rehmeyer, aged 60.

"Hexed!"

"Be-witched!"

"Lock of hair."

"The *Long Lost Friend*."

Again and again did the above words issue from the counsel for John H. Blymyer, and again and again did the defendant speak those words in all the seriousness that any man could who believed as did John Blymyer.

John Blymyer, thirty-two or three years of age, born of the most humble sort of parents, the boy without a chance to make good because his brain would not grow; the boy with mental apparitions of "witches" and the like, is going to spend the rest of his life in the penitentiary—HAPPY; not so much because he killed a man, but because he "broke the spell" that had been placed on him by the man he is said to have killed, and from the moment of the killing he has felt himself to be a better man, in that he can now "eat, sleep and rest better," and the "witches" cannot bother him anymore, nor can any "spell" be again placed on him!

Poor John, the child with faith—but faith in the unseen, and unfelt things in life—in his delusions, hallucinations and illusions.

Who killed poor Cock Robin?

"Who killed Nelson D. Rehmeyer" in a lonely farm house set apart in a sparsely settled part of York county?

"I didn't kill him," said John Blymyer.

"Why did you go to Rehmeyer's house then, if not to kill him?"

"I went there to get a lock of hair, or the book called the *Long Lost Friend.*"

"What did you want with the lock of hair, or the *Long Lost Friend?*"

"To break a "spell" that Rehmeyer had put on me, and Curry, and the Hess family."

"When you killed him, did that break the spell?"

"Yes."

"Do you feel better?"

"Yes. Now I can eat, and sleep, and rest better, and I am not pining away."

And John Blymyer, who sat, a defendant on the witness' stand, during the trial that meant liberty, or death, or at least life imprisonment for him, yawned, time after time, as he told his story, in a quiet, dispassionate and straightforward manner. And at 7.40 o'clock p. m., of the third day of the now famous trial, the defendant, John Blymyer, heard the fateful words from the foreman of the jury, "Guilty of murder in the first degree, with the recommendation of life imprisonment."

So it is that Blymyer will pay the penalty of his crime; but does he care? Hear John a few minutes after the sentence had been told him: "I am happy now. I am not bewitched any more. I can sleep and eat and I am not pining away." And after a short pause continued, "But I think that they went a little strong. Yes, that's it—a little too strong."

———

"Every event is the son of its own father," was perhaps never more apropos than in the case of the Commonwealth vs. John Blymyer.

Had John Blymyer been born and lived in the present era, he would have been like almost any other rational youth of his day and age. But John wasn't the thirty-two or three years of age, as he is said to be. John Blymyer, the son of Emanuel Blymyer, aged about 60, with no particular place to call his home, was "born" ages and ages ago (figuratively speaking). Emanuel and John Blymyer, father and son; the mother, as well as others of the children in said family were "born" so far back in the ages, that it is hardly conceivable that jurisdiction could be had over either of them, in the common recourse at law! The Blymyers are "throw-backs" from the early ages of history, if one may judge by appearances, and hearing.

Emanuel Blymyer, who is not sure of his age, but is high in the fifties, or already in his sixties, still counts, and indicates the number of his children by raising his hand and showing two, three or four fingers; we verily believe that if one were to ask him a question that would involve more than ten units, or digits, that no answer would be forthcoming, for we have doubts whether Emanuel can reckon higher than the ten digits normal man is equipped with.

Emanuel Blymyer, on the witness stand, testified that he lived at three places, telling where they were, and that he made baskets in order to procure money enough to keep body and soul together. He cannot read, nor write, and we suspect that his witness' oath "went over his head." But Blymyer, the father, as a witness for his son, was just as straight-forward and honest as a man could be, and with the son, made two of the best witnesses on the stand during the three days' trial.

We stated that the Blymyers were "throw-backs" from the middle or dark ages, and the reader will know then what is meant by such statement. While they are here in the flesh with their fellowman in 1929, their thoughts are not. Their thoughts are far, far away. As a basket-maker, the elder Blymyer; and as a chronic loafer, under his delusions, John, the son, portray to us living examples of the kind of people who inhabited the sparsely settled parts of the earth in the times of the Middle Ages.

Emanuel Blymyer, when questioned, said: "One of my daughters diedt; she—wass—well—anyway dere was somedings da matter wis da headt. And I'm dat way, too, sometimes." He repeated several times that "John was sick, too, and couldn't work, and dere wass somedings da matter wis hiss headt," and that John was "hexed."

One swift glance at Emanuel Blymyer would satisfy the average person as to the type and calibre of man he is. His dress is that of the man "in rags." His speech that of the man who speaks little, and who knows little to speak. His hair, not all gray by any means, have probably not seen a brush or comb for years and years, if ever. Nor can we believe that the body, or clothes ever see cleansing. As to the birth of Emanuel Blymyer, belated from the Middle Ages to about 1870, we can only hazard a guess. Picturing his arrival into this world, one must almost suppose that from his present appearance, he had a mighty deplorable entrance. We can hardly imagine a regular physician in the 1870's attending the arrival of Emanuel Blymyer, but that he did overcome some obstacles placed in his way by nature, and eventually take unto himself a mate, is apparent.

In the course of his life with his mate, he has become the parent of seven children, one dying, as stated previously. All these children have been the off-spring of a parent who for all his life has been a back-woodsman, and who has lived in an almost primitive state all this time; a parent who "knew his witches," and who, instead of making the "best" of life, seems to have made out of it the most miserable failure.

One must wonder who is responsible for "failures" like these. That is difficult to tell; society is quite complex, but has a part in the progress of mankind, or lack of it. And Emanuel Blymyer and his son John are excellent examples of what happens when nature is allowed to take its course. Where the generations previous to the two mentioned came from, or what they were, we have no means of knowing, but the intelligence comes to us that these people were never known to be among any of the active type of woodsmen, or farm folk. They have for generations, apparently, been of the "backward type," and as so often is the case, inter-marriages, and cohabitings, and common law affairs with these poorer classes, "play the devil" in our courts of justice, and with society generally. Witness the frequent intermingling of the same blood and mental types, and the pouring out of mental defectives.

Where, in the history of criminal trials, has there ever been a case where the obtaining of a "lock of hair, or a *Pow Wow* book" have been such inconceivable and impossible motives for murder?

Like begets like, and we see the weak John Blymyer, the son of equally mentally and physically weak parents. For John there is no struggle for existence in his life. His outlook, and vision of life cannot be seen through the eyes of the average person, but must be seen through eyes representing the kind of people living during the dark ages. Deductions as to John's mental apparitions would not be mentioned here if expert medical testimony and tests had not been made at different times in John's life, proving his stupidness, ignorance, or incompatibility; his hallucinations. His father, on the stand, admitted also having certain beliefs in witches, and the like, and the son has inherited these beliefs, with interest.

There is no effort necessary to picture John Blymyer as an unwanted child; did you ever observe the really poor people who *wanted* children, and still more children? Generally speaking, they do not want them, but they get them just the same, and the larger the crop, the greater the difficulties and annoyances resultant upon society as a whole. Society, the law, the State, the nation, are responsible in no small degree for such children of fate and nature, as we see in John Blymyer's life. John was clothed neatly enough at the trial, and to all ordinary appearances was like any other chap of like age and environment in the community. To look at him one would scarcely suppose, or even believe if told by some other person, that John believed in "witches," and believed so with all his heart and mind.

But John had an hereditary handicap; he was born with foolish ideas in his head, if a child ever has ideas at birth. Certainly John grew up like his father, and it was inevitable fate that in going out into the world, even away from his own folks, and acquiring ever so little knowledge from day to day, that John should meet with difficulties. His persistent delusions from childhood, up into manhood, had so unnerved him that he could scarcely work, or eat, or sleep, or do any thing, but worry.

Time came, that John was sent to the County Home of York county, where he was examined as to his sanity, and upon its outcome, John was ordered committed to the State Hospital for the Insane, at Harrisburg. In 1923, when about twenty-six years of age, he was brought to the Hospital, at Harrisburg, and after 48 days "residence" there, effected his escape.

Before his confinement to the State institution, any number of symptoms of a sort of mental derangement, or insanity, were apparent to any number of persons acquainted with John Blymyer. John lived under the apprehension that he was ill, and pining away; that witches were after him, and that he was "hexed." For years, in his early childhood, he had lived in proximity, and at times had worked for Nelson D. Rehmeyer, reputed "witch-doctor," now deceased. Blymyer suffered these hallucinations and delusions for days and years, and seemingly nothing could be done to alleviate the mental depression that was his as a result of his beliefs. These ideas of John's were as persistent as they could be— as persistent as the day follows the night.

Expert testimony brought out on the stand was to the effect that John suffered mental beliefs for which there was no certain, or likely cure; that John wasn't sick physically, but that he wasn't well mentally. The experts testified that their examinations showed that John knew some matters of of history (beginner's), and could distinguish between some incidents or others, but when the question of witches was put to him by the experts, he remained firm in his attitude. The witches were after him, and from this he would not budge one iota. He was "hexed!" He testified that he had visited nearly every doctor in York at some time or other, and had sought treatments from every possible source for the relief that he desired from the witches which were "sapping his life away." He once took electric treatments, he testified.

John even sought out the pow-pow doctors, and went to possibly a dozen of them in late years, one of them being a colored man; and several of them being women. With these pan-handlers, (for most of them seem to have accepted fees from John for their "treatment" of his illness,) he seems to have found his source of satisfaction. For all of those to whom he went for pow-wow treatments told him the same thing. He probably told them of his condition, his belief in and fear of witches, and asked them whether there was anything like that the matter with him. Of course all of them had the idea all right—they agreed with John, and said that he was "hexed." And for this information John paid out from $1.00 to $5.00, and sometimes $10.00, per consultation.

If this young man had had just a small grain of common-sense, he could have distinguished the difference in his case, as diagnosed by the experts, and that of the pan-handlers; but he had his own ideas of what ailed him, and the ones who agreed with him were the ones he sought. And one day he went to a Mrs. Emma Noll, said to live at Marietta; a woman of some ninety years, according to reports. On the witness stand John testified, and apparently with no hesitancy or mental-reservation, that Mrs. Noll told him who it was that had him bewitched. This probably was the first person to go so far with John's imagination, and from that time his mind seems to have become more determined than ever, that he was "hexed," and he suggested to several other persons, involved in this same trial, that they were bewitched, and by the same man who had him at his mercy.

In a case like this one, it seems ever so reasonable to suppose that John didn't know, and didn't realize fully, even though he was thirty-two, that to take a life (if this ever did occur to him before the crime was committed)—was unlawful. He believed in self-preservation as the first law of nature (a lowly animal instinct); and his apparitions were that Rehmeyer had him bewitched, and was thus undermining his health, and that he was thereby slowly, but surely, being brought to his death by the influences and control of the older man, over him.

The visit to Mrs. Noll, seems to have been the first and most important development in his years of effort to shake off the spell. Here he was told how he could find out who had him betwitched, and she is furthermore said to have told him who it was. Mrs. Noll asked John to give her some paper money, if he had any, to perform her magical feat of discovering to John who the real witch might be. Handing a dollar-bill to Mrs. Noll, the latter smoothed it out nicely and laid it on the palm of Blymyer's left hand. He was told to concentrate his thoughts on the object before him, and that upon the removal of the bill, he would see the picture of the man who had him bewitched, on the palm of his hand! Doing this, he was greeted with the likeness of Nelson D. Rehmeyer! This John claims to have beheld in his hand as plain as could be, and Mrs. Noll asked him if he knew Rehmeyer, to which he assented, and he claims that Mrs. Noll told him that Rehmeyer was the man.

————

The court was trying John Blymyer, as one of three boys, whom the Commonwealth charged with the killing of Rehmeyer. But who killed Rehmeyer? Did Blymyer, Hess, or Curry? Or, did "society" kill him? Or was the Commonwealth of Pennsylvania a contributor to the crime, in that it permitted an apparently insane man to be at large? Did Mrs. Noll, as a possible accessory before the fact have anything to do with the killing? Did she have any grudge against Rehmeyer? Is she not said to have put the words or thoughts in John's mind?

Did John know before he went to Mrs. Noll's *who* had him "hexed." Apparently not; and it was not long after he had heard who it was that was slowly killing him, that Blymyer learned *how* it was possible to break the spell! The same Mrs. Noll, Blymyer testified, told him that in order to break the spell, it would be necessary to obtain a lock of hair from Rehmeyer's head, or his copy of the *Long Lost Friend*. And so John rolled over in his feeble mind, the idea that Rehmeyer had him "hexed," and that to obtain relief and freedom of the spell, he *would* obtain a lock of hair, and the *Long Lost Friend*.

One should not lose sight of the fact that Blymyer, when a patient at the State Hospital for the Insane, was considered a lunatic. After his escape from the institution, he went back to York county, and more or less during the year following escape, the Hospital authorities made efforts to locate him, but without avail. When he reached home, he quarreled with his wife, with whom he had three children, and who subsequently divorced Blymyer. But as a result of the attempted killing of his wife, by shooting, he was arrested on some minor charge, and sentenced to the York county jail for a time. Here he was said to have exhibited all the symptoms of a man mentally deranged, or mentally deficient. The State Hospital authorities did not know that he was imprisoned while they were making their search, and under a State law, one who escapes from an institution for the insane, and has managed to avoid arrest for a period of a year, is accounted for on the records of the hospital, as being "discharged"—*but not cured!* John, therefore, may be presumed to have been just as much deranged mentally four or five years after having effected his escape, and at the time the crime was committed, as at any time previous, or even more so under the nervous tension of gaining his "spell breakers;" but the law is the law, and evidence must be produced that is bona fide, and substantial, to prove a contention. And here John's case was weak — the chain lacked several important links, and gaps in his past that might have proved of value to him in showing him to have been insane from birth to now, unfortunately were missing. But we must return to the motive or incidents in John's life, from the time Mrs. Noll is said to have put certain ideas into his head, up to the time of the crime.

It appears from the evidence that John saw other pow-wow doctors after seeing Mrs. Noll, but that no one else, at any time, ever told him that Rehmeyer had him "hexed." though they did say that he was bewitched. How to break the spell, came solely from Mrs. Noll, and to break that spell, to sustain, and regain lost health, and probably avoid death, was uppermost in John's thoughts.

By the mere habit of living John had become able to make a sort of livelihood as a cigar maker. There was nothing apparently the matter with John's health, he functioned normally in every way, it seems, except mentally. In the course of his employment not long before the murder of Rehmeyer, Blymyer met John Curry, a 14-year-old lad, who looks to be 19, and who had missed school in York, and joined a branch of the army on the strength of his apparent age. John Curry, whose father died when John was a lad of but 5 years or so, is another of those unfortunate poor, who " just grew up." Children like this cannot truly be said to have had the same chance as those whose parents are living, and who are better off. The deplorable fact about such instances as this is, that the State or community, so seldom takes a personal, or what would be something similar to a "fatherly interest," in such orphaned tots. Any one who is willing to let his thoughts drift back to about the year 1914, when nearly the whole world was set on fire by war, can see the vast strides that have been made in all walks of life in these last 15 years. Hand in hand with progress, went poverty, and temptation of every sort. What John Curry's home life was like, is unknown to the writer, but it is sufficient for the point we have in mind, to say that any child, deprived of its male parent, from 1914 up to this time, had as hard a time walking the straight and narrow path, as any child in the history of the world has ever had. This world is pleasure mad; money mad; lustful and greedy. John Curry was born into this atmosphere, and with a drunkard for a step-father, and always neglected, it would not surprise us to learn that his mind, too, was of the visionary and impressionistic type.

Blymyer and Curry met and formed a friendship, under a mutual belief that something was the matter with each other, and that they both knew that they were bewitched. Curry did not know who had bewitched him, until Blymyer told him. This was said to have been Rehmeyer, who is described by his widow, as being an "old devilish witch." These two, young man, and boy, later on met the family of Milton G. Hess, and here Blymyer again attributed illness in the Hess family and trouble on their farm, to the "witch" spell that Nelson Rehmeyer had placed on that family, same as Rehmeyer had placed on Curry and himself. Enter Wilbert G. Hess, 18 years old, into the case, who met Blymyer for the first time in his life, on Sunday, November 25, 1928, just two days before the crime was committed.

Of a somewhat better-looking class and type of citizens, (but believers in witchcraft, etc., just the same), the Hess family, probably entirely innocent of the character of Blymyer, were entangled in less than no time in the horrible affair that has caused them untold sorrow, and nation-wide, if not world-wide publicity, in newspapers, magazines, books and "gossip."

Here we have the mention of three persons who claim to have had certain ailments or complaints, and each of them was led to think, and actually believed that they were suffering as a result of spells that had been put on them. To shake off these spells hovering over all of them, Blymyer proposed at the home of the Hess family, in York township, York county, on Sunday, November 25, that arrangements be made to go to Rehmeyer's, in the Hess automobile, to obtain the lock of hair, or the book, the *Long Lost Friend*.

Accordingly, on Monday evening, November 26, Clayton G. Hess, who is a foreman in the lumber yard of Hess Brothers, at Gramley, left his work in his automobile, going to the wire cloth factory, where he met his wife. With her he went to East Princess street, near the city market, and there they picked up Blymyer, alias John Albright, and Curry, alias John Russell. From there they drove down the Susquehanna trail in the Hess automobile to Hametown, and turned left on a road near the church. They traveled this road about two and a half miles, to a woods. There Hess left Blymyer and Curry and returned to York.

Clayton Hess on the witness stand declared that Blymyer had explained that he "has to go down and get some of the man's hair, because Rehmeyer had a spell over my father and mother. Blymyer said he has to be there until Friday or Saturday, and when he gets the hair he would see my father and mother in market (at York). He said he must get the hair and dig a hole 6 or 8 feet deep and bury it."

It appears from the testimony, that Blymyer and Curry were the welcome guests of Rehmeyer on the night in question, being Monday. Tuesday was the "big night," and of that we shall write later.

It is proper, at this time, to point out that Curry and Blymyer had intended to procure the lock of hair, or the book, themselves, and prepared for that purpose with a reasonably stout piece of cotton rope for some purpose or another, not fully explained, but presumably to tie Rehmeyer while they "snipped" the lock of hair. Frank Lahr, a clerk in Swartz's store, at South George street and College avenue, pointed out Blymyer, as the man who came into the store with another (Curry), and bought 25 feet of cotton rope. Three pieces of rope, taken from the charred body of Rehmeyer, were presented as evidence in court, and upon examination with a piece which came from the same spool as purchased from by Blymyer and Curry, were found to tally.

One of the first witnesses to testify was Mrs. Alice Rehmeyer, widow of the deceased Nelson Rehmeyer. She testified that he was 60 years and one month of age, on the night he met his death. While there was no animosity between the widow and the deceased, the two lived on their separate farms, a mile or so apart, and visited each other occasionally. On the night of the murder Mrs. Rehmeyer states, that Blymyer, whom she knew since he was a child, and who was raised in her neighborhood, and another companion, by the name of John (Curry), came to her place at 7.45 in the evening. They asked whether Rehmeyer was there, to which she replied that he was not, so after a visit of a half hour or thereabouts, the young men started across fields to the Nelson Rehmeyer home. This night, being Monday, was spent at Rehmeyer's, as a guest of the old man, whom the widow just a short while before is said to have called "an old devilish witch," that she hoped wouldn't come over to see her anymore.

Tuesday evening, Blymyer and Curry again called at the Hess home, and asked that they be again taken to the Rehmeyer home, and that if possible some one else of the Hess family, should go along, because the old man was pretty strong and they needed more help to get the lock of hair. Accordingly Clayton Hess took them, and his brother Wilbert, aged 18, to the same place as on the night before, this place being the woods, from where the trio walked to the lonely cabin in the dark of the evening.

The records of the trial show that the three boys abovementioned, went to the home of the witch doctor for the express purpose of procuring a lock of hair, or a book;

their preparations seem to have been slight; all that they are said to have had was 25 feet of cotton rope. No concealed deadly weapons, or the like, figure in the case, previous to the commission of the crime.

Various experts were called to testify as to the insanity of Blymyer, who was tried separately, as was each of the other defendants. County and city officials, too, were witnesses for the Commonwealth, and the defense relied almost entirely on the fact that "insanity" would save Blymyer from a first-degree verdict. The trial appeared serious enough throughout, and few occasions were observed for more than a little smile, as certain facts developed. However, one instance was enjoyed by all present who heard it, and it but goes to show the type of persons being tried.

On the stand was Oscar Altland, superintendent of the County Home of York county, where Blymyer had at one time been an inmate, and from which place he was sent, in 1923, to the Asylum at Harrisburg. Testifying, as one of those who had seen Blymyer, and observed his actions, for from one to two years before the commission of the crime, Mr. Altland said that Blymyer had called at the County Home in 1927. He then asked for medical assistance, and was advised by Altland to see a doctor. Blymyer told him that he was taking medicine at the time.

"What is it?" asked Altland.

"Lydia Pinkham's," said Blymyer, who was thereupon advised to go to work. But Blymyer said he "couldn't work, because the witches were after him." This occasioned the only really humorous incident of the trial.

Much of the time of the trial was consumed in making "offers" to prove by this witness or that witness, certain peculiarities which could be deduced to indicate the defendant insane. The court ruled time and time again that no testimony by lay witnesses would be admitted, as to the condition of John Blymyer's mind three or four years, or even two years before the crime was committed. The court held that under the law, the State and the law demanded to know the condition, or state of mind of the defendant at, or about, the time of the commission of the crime.

The body of Rehmeyer was found about noon of Thanksgiving Day, the discovery being made by David Vanover, a neighbor. The stock on the farm had not been tended, as usual, and their lowing, had caused Vanover to call at the farm to inquire if anything was wrong. He described to the court and jury, his observation of the dead man, as he was discovered lying on the floor. Dr. William C. Langston, York, described the condition of the body as he found it when called by Deputy Coroner Dr. W. H. Schellhamer. He said that Rehmeyer was lying on the floor face downward, his feet bent upright from the knees at an angle of about 90 degrees. The feet were tied at the ankles. At the side of the body were found an oil lamp, with the burner off, a flash-light, a snap off a halter rope, and pieces of broken chair. Parts of clothing and substances like straw or excelsior, all burned, were on top of the body. The body was severely burned on the back, thighs and legs. There were cuts and bruises on the head, one of which was a compound fracture of the skull, and which, in his opinion, might have caused the death of Rehmeyer.

Dr. L. U. Zech, county coroner, gave similar testimony, and identified pieces of burned clothing, etc. John Wagner, undertaker, Shrewsbury, also identified articles taken from the body.

Detectives testified against the defendant, and all in all, the case of the Commonwealth vs. John Blymyer, looked bad for John. The defendant's witnesses were either disqualified, or were not able to appear, and his counsel, Herbert B. Cohen, appointed by the county for the defense, was finally compelled to put the defendant on the stand as a witness in his own behalf.

We don't believe that a witness, and especially a defendant in a murder trial, ever sat on a witness stand with such calmness and indifference in manner as did John Blymyer. He positively yawned from time to time, as his counsel questioned him, and as the district attorney, Amos W. Herrmann, cross-examined him. The import of it all made no more impression on him than it did on the clock on the opposite end of the room, and which was all that one could hear besides John's low voice, and that of his counsel. The spectators were afraid at first that John might talk too much. Perhaps he did, but while he spoke, unhesitatingly telling of his part in the affairs, no sign of emotion, no moistening of his lips, no squirming about in the chair, no twitching, showed on John Blymyer. No personal interest in the affair whatever; so far as John was concerned, the snap of a finger might be said to be his interest in the whole affair. Could any sane and sound man sit there between court and jury, in the seat of the person to be judged, and show so little concern? No; only one whose shallow mind does not grasp all important things, would show so little concern. John was either insane—or the calmest actor to ever face death!

A personal interview with one of the experts who figured in the trial brings out another important phase. This professional man interviewed Blymyer before the trial, and during the course of their conversation John stated that the object of the visit to the Rehmeyer home was solely to secure the hair or the book. On further questioning, he denied having planned extreme measures in order to secure the objects of their visit. John denied that they had ever entertained any thoughts of killing the older man. But he was stout, and muscular, and the boys would be mere puppets in the event of there being trouble to get what they wanted. This plan was "robbery"—of an unusual sort; not one for gain for themselves, or others; but one that was absolutely necessary to break a spell—to save a life! Do other robbers and thieves stoop to a level of securing such as an unkempt lock of hair, or a second-hand and much used pow-wow book with no potential value? Does the reader not see that this kind of robbery is in a class by itself? The upshot of the whole being that in endeavoring to procure what they wanted, these boys, by mere accident, due to overzealousness, got the old man too much upset and thus started a "free-for-all." Rehmeyer met his death accidentally it is believed, for Blymyer made a remark to a confidant before the trial to that effect. John was surprised during the general encounter and at one stage of it cried out: "My God, he's dead." This remark makes one feel sure that such an end was not premeditated—but that having started the action, it became a case of Rehmeyer vs. the three.

The old man probably did not fully comprehend or understand that they merely wanted a lock of hair, or his book, and defended himself, as he would against common thugs, with the result that is now known to the world.

Let us put John on the stand and hear his testimony:

"John, how old are you?"
John replied promptly, but in a low tone of voice.
"Thirty-three."
"You'll have to talk louder, John," said his attorney.

"Thirty-three."

"No, the jury can't hear you."

"Thirty-three."

"How many brothers and sisters have you?"

Blymyer counted over his fingers, replying directly:

"Four sisters and two brothers."

"All living?"

"All except one."

"Know what she died of?" John moved his hands, bringing one of them across the forehead.

"Sick in the head," he replied.

"For the past ten years, how have you been feeling?"

"I couldn't rest or sleep; I couldn't talk."

John's fingers seemed to be a part of his manner in directing his speech, and he had them moving quite freely during the time he was on the stand. When he spoke of being unable to talk, his fingers moved up to his mouth.

"What caused you to feel that way, John?"

"I was bewitched."

This question was felt by the defense counsel to be the big point in the case. John replied in a manner that betrayed no emotion—he showed no more concern over that remark than if he had been holding a conversation about the weather.

"Did you see any doctors?"

"Yes, Dr. Lenhart;" (reputed pow-wow doctor).

"No, I mean real doctors. Any real doctors?"

The defendant named half a dozen or more doctors in York, whom, he said, he had consulted.

"Were you ever treated in the York Hospital?"

"Yes, sir."

"Did you feel this way when you were living with your wife?"

"Yes, sir."

"What did the doctors say was the matter with you?"

"You mean the medical doctors? Well, they said I had a nervous disease. They said I had melancholia."

"Did they help you?"

The reply to the above question did not seem to be just what Counsel Cohen expected, so he tried another query.

"Did you feel any better after you saw them?"

"No, not much."

"After you went to the medical doctors, John, you went to Dr. Lenhart?"

"Yes."

"What did he say was the matter with you?"

"He said I was bewitched."

The tone still continued calm, and even, as could be.

"Who else treated you?"

"Sam Schmuck."

"How many times did you see Sam Schmuck?"

"About a dozen."

"Did you feel any better after you saw him?"

"No."

"What did Schmuck say was the matter with you?"

"He said I was bewitched."

"How many times did you see Mrs. Noll?" (Mrs. Noll, said to be the Marietta "witch," is said to be in her nineties, and to have wielded much influence over Blymyer).

"Oh, quite a few times."

"What did she tell you was the matter with you?"

"She said I was bewitched."

"What did you say to her when you first saw her?"

"She asked me first how I felt and I said that's why I came here to ask how I felt. Then she told me that somebody was keeping my rest from me; that I couldn't sleep or eat and was pining away."

"And you believed you were pining away?"

"Yes, sir."

"You believed you were dying?"

"Yes, sir, I was."

"Did Mrs. Noll tell you who had bewitched you?"

"Yes, she said a gentleman down in the country. She said Rehmeyer, and I said which Rehmeyer, and she said 'Nelson Rehmeyer.' "

Now the trend of questioning changed, and Cohen asked how Mrs. Noll operated in her discovery of who had him bewitched. Blymyer had spoken of a dollar bill, so Cohen produced a bank note which he handed to John, telling him to indicate the way Mrs. Noll did. Blymyer took the note, and placed it on the palm of his left hand, and looked up.

"She put it on my hand this way," he said. "Then she said some words and took it off and I looked down in my hand and there in my hand I could see Nelson Rehmeyer."

"What did you say then?"

"I asked her what would break the spell and she said get the book, the *Long Lost Friend*, or the lock of hair."

"Did she know Rehmeyer had such a book?"

"She must have, she told me to get the book."

"How many times did you go back to see Mrs. Noll?"

"Five or six times."

"Did she always tell you Nelson Rehmeyer had bewitched you?"

"Yes, but that was the first time I saw him in my hand."

"When was this?"

"May be about three months ago. Something like that."

"Did anyone else ever tell you Nelson Rehmeyer had you hexed?"

"No, sir."

"After Mrs. Noll, did you see any other powwow doctors?"

"Yes, Lenhart and Schmuck."

"Did they tell you who had bewitched you?"

"No, they said I was bewitched, but they said they weren't sure who did it."

"Did you ever go to a pow-wow doctor named Murray?" (Rufus Murray, negro).

"Yes."

"Did he say you were bewitched?"

"Yes, sir."

"When did you see him?"

"Not for about a year."

"When you saw Rehmeyer's picture in your hand, you knew he had bewitched you?"

"Yes, sir; she (Mrs. Noll) told me so."

Cohen then asked Blymyer regarding his acquaintance with Milton Hess, father of Wilbert, the 18-year-old boy, who happened to be one of the principals in the murder of Rehmeyer. The elder Hess had told Blymyer about numerous troubles within the family, and on the farm; crops were failing, cattle were dying; the family was ill, and the next time John went to see Mrs. Noll, he asked her about it.

Cohen then continued: "What did she tell you about the Hess family?"

"She told me they were bewitched."

"Did you work for him?"

"Yes, I used to dig his potatoes."

"Did you ever go to Nelson Rehmeyer's for pow-wow treatment?"

"Yes."

"When?"

"When I was down about a year ago."

"When you went there, did you sleep in the house?"

"The first time I did. The second time I came home."

"Now, John, I want you to come down to the time just before all this happened and tell us how you decided to go to Rehmeyer's house and for what purpose."

"Well, John Curry (the 14-year-old lad implicated) and I talked it over and him and I made out to get hair or the book."

"What did Curry say?"

"He said we could get some rope and tie Rehmeyer up and get the hair, but I said that we better use wire; he said it will cut, so we decided to get some rope at Swartz's store, then we went to Curry's home."

As explained, this occurred on Monday, November 29, the day before the murder; and on this same evening the boys were at the home of Mrs. Alice Rehmeyer, as had been testified.

"Monday evening John (Curry) and I went to the Hess home and we talked to Wilbert and asked his brother, Clayton Hess, if he would take us where we were going in his car. We went to Rehmeyer's house and when he got there he wasn't there so we went and saw Mrs. Rehmeyer. I asked her where he was, but she didn't know. I asked her didn't he ever come over, and she said yes, he did, and she wished the old devilish witch wouldn't come over. Then we went back to Rehmeyer's and saw a light and he let us in. I asked if he had a book called the *Long Lost Friend,* and he said he had. That was all he said, you know, just that he had it. So when we asked if we could stay all night he said all right."

"You slept in Rehmeyer's home Monday night, all night?"

"Yes, sir; in the kitchen; and so did John Curry."

"Where did Rehmeyer sleep?"

"I don't know; he went upstairs and turned off the light and in the morning he got up and made breakfast and we ate."

"Why didn't you tie him up and get the hair that night?"

"We made out he was too much for us to throw down and we made out to get Wilbert Hess to help us get the hair."

"What happened at Hess's on Tuesday?"

"Nothing much. We asked Clayton to take us down and he did. And we took Wilbert to help get the hair or the book."

"Did you tell Clayton what you were going for?"

"Yes."

"Did you tell Wilbert?"

"Yes."

"Did you tell Mrs. Hess?"

"Not that I can remember of."

Blymyer next launched into a description of the fatal visit to Rehmeyer's home on the night of the crime. He denied taking active part in the slaying; claimed he had not struck Rehmeyer, except with his fist; had not strangled him, nor lighted the match with which the body was set on fire and partly consumed.

"All right, John; tell us more," said his counsel.

"We went down to the same place and went to Rehmeyer's home, and rapped at the door and Rehmeyer opened the window and asked who was there. I said I came for the book and he said he'd come down. We went in and he was holding a lamp. I said where was the book and he didn't say anything. He went to the table to put away the flashlight and Hess and I grabbed him. I started to beat him with my fists. I grabbed a chair and hit at him, but I missed and the chair hit the floor and broke. We got him down and he said to let him up and he'd get the book, so we let him up and he came for me full force like this." Blymyer illustrated with his hands, extended forward like claws. Still no emotion in his voice. "Hess and Curry grabbed him and they started to beat him. Then Curry gets a block of wood and hits Rehmeyer with it twice. Curry dropped the wood and walked around Rehmeyer and kicked him in the stomach."

"Was there any blood?" inquired his attorney.

"Yes, sir, when Curry hit him."

"How did the blood make you feel?"

"The blood made me feel sick."

"How did you feel?"

"Well, sick; like I wanted to vomit; you know." Here John's recollections make him again make several motions with his hands, and an expression on his face that indicated a sickening feeling.

"What happened then?"

"Curry grabbed the lamp and went upstairs and Hess behind him, and I went, too."

"Why did you go?"

"To look for the book."

Then followed a description of the scene upstairs, as he told how Curry and Hess had found money on a dresser and how they pocketed it.

[21]

"Did you say anything to them about taking the money?"

"I told them they oughtn't to do that."

After returning from the upstairs, and going to the place where Rehmeyer lay, Curry is said to have tied a rope around Rehmeyer's neck. Blymyer said he poured water around the body, because someone has mentioned fingerprints. Later on in his testimony he declared that he did not know what was meant by fingerprints.

"Well, go on, John."

"Hessy got the tick off the bed and put it on Rehmeyer. And then Curry takes the lamp and pours oil on the mattress. And he asks me have I got a match and I say no I don't smoke and I haven't got no matches. So then John finds a match and he struck it and threw it down and then we went out. He went first, then Curry, and then me. We all started running across the field because I thought I saw some one standing in the road, but Curry said it was just a shadow."

After the continuation for some little time, of questions and answers, neither the defendant nor his counsel seemed to show any signs of tiring. The whole time during which Blymyer was on the stand he was as rhythmic and as steady as is "A. B. C." to the educated man.

The Judge, too, was kept quite busy during the questioning of Blymyer, as he made numerous notes. All parley between the Judge and the prosecuting attorney and counsel for the defense having ceased with John's inimitable demeanor on the stand. Then followed a unique series of questions.

"John, could you put a spell on me?" said Mr. Cohen.

"No, sir; I couldn't."

"Could you put a spell on anyone?"

"No."

"Could Mrs. Noll put a spell on anyone?"

"I don't know."

"If Rehmeyer were alive could he put a spell on me?"

"Yes, he could."

"Since Rehmeyer and his hair have been buried, do you feel better?"

"Yes, I can sleep and rest and eat."

"You are building yourself up, are you?"

"Well, I feel stronger."

John seems to have been quite satisfied with his lot, even though he had been in the county jail for over a month at the time of the trial. He wore rather a picture of contentment. That such were the reflections in his mind may be noted in what at any other time would be considered very "bold" statements.

"John, would you kill anyone who had hexed you?"

"Yes."

"If the Judge of this Court put a spell on you, would you kill him?"

"Yes."

"If the District Attorney put a spell on you, would you kill him?"

"Yes."

"If your father put a spell on you would you kill him?"

"Yes."

Then came the cross-examination of a determined District Attorney. This failed to move the defendant.

"Did you receive any money from Milton Hess?" District Attorney Hermann asked.

"Yes."

"How much?"

"Ten dollars."

"Why?"

"To get him a Queen Elizabeth root from Sam Schmuck to keep away the hexes."

"Did you make Milton Hess believe you had the power to remove spells?"

"No, sir."

The cross-examination concerned itself chiefly with the State's effort to establish the robbery motive. Blymyer admitted that Rehmeyer had taken some object from his pocket during the fight and handed it to Curry, but he said the object might have been the *Long Lost Friend* which Mrs. Noll had told him to burn.

———

Blymyer, after the conclusion of his testimony, was taken back to his seat with his counsel, and then began the final battle to save him from the chair. His counsel made a fervent plea before the jury. The district attorney, contending that the motive of robbery and the subsequent outcome, demanded that the jury find the defendant guilty as charged. Following the charge by Judge Ray P. Sherwood, the jury retired, took three ballots, and reached their verdict in a little over two hours.

"Guilty of murder in the first degree, with the recommendation of life imprisonment."

So ended the trial of John Blymyer, "born" in the Middle Ages, and whose actual living had been postponed to the Twentieth Century, A. D.

The law has been appeased; the public is satisfied. Expressions have even been heard that the deceased was none too good to meet the end he did. The lock of hair—all of the hair, in fact, now lies under six or eight feet of ground!

The newspapers have ceased their sensational accounts of the trial, as they appeared from day to day; the reporters and photographers have returned to their assignments in their own metropolitan areas. The shades in the court room have been drawn, and John Blymyer is a ward of the State. He will spend the rest of his days in the penitentiary—*happy!* Now he can "eat, and sleep, and rest better." He is no longer bewitched.

————

There are murder trials and murder trials, but few like this one. Had not the imaginary, mysterious, elusive enigma of witchcraft, pow-wowism, voodooism, "hex" and the like, been injected into the case————

But it was!

Immediately big news!

The metropolitan papers, wallowing deep in mire of their own, thought this would prove to be a "witch trial" of no mean importance!

Reporters from all papers and press associations; features played up in all papers until the day of the trial, and then overdone!

An apparently insane man implicated in the killing of one no better than himself!

John Blymyer, as a space-grafter, has been the best bet, non-politically, since Lindbergh crossed the Atlantic!

The people of York and York county were as little concerned and ruffled about this trial as one could well imagine. Very few people from York attended the various sessions during the trial; most of those present being persons awaiting their call for jury duty in another court, witnesses, and reporters. (A "tip" to reporters who in the future are disappointed in not getting "reserved seats" at trials that have all the "ear marks" of being sensational:—"make friends;" don't come into Pennsylvania courts of justice with a "chip on your shoulder," and a determination to "raise hell" in your "sheet" about the judge, or the trial itself.)

The case was but an unfortunate one, which might have happened in any rural section anywhere in the United States, or the entire world. It could easily have occurred in New York City, or Washington! But York happens to have been the victim of circumstances, as was John Blymyer, and the only echo York county will recall will be John's board bill!

The populace of York county are not "dumb" and ignorant, as some papers would have their readers believe, just because of the fact that many of their people are Pennsylvania-Germans. On the contrary, York, the City, is one large manufacturing centre, products being made there reaching every point of the globe worthy of mention.

This history of the trial of John Blymyer, tends to portray a layman's view of the complex situation surrounding a deplorable circumstance. This article is not prepared with a view to filling a demand from a newspaper for "so much space," but is prepared by the author as a matter of historical interest for the future. None of the actors in the drama were known to him. The newspapers bearing an account of the trial daily, which vied with each other as to which one would carry the most sensational stories, will soon have been forgotten or destroyed, while this article of the trial, preserved in an attractive manner, may last for years and may serve at least as a word lesson to others. There are no mercenary or other motives underlying this account of the life of John Blymyer, and the ultimate outcome of the practice of such as believe as he believed, and practice as he "dreamed."

Who killed Cock Robin?

"Who killed Nelson D. Rehmeyer?"

"I didn't," said John Blymyer; "nor I," said John Curry; "nor I," said Wilbert Hess.

The Commonwealth of Pennsylvania says the three just mentioned killed Rehmeyer. The Commonwealth, dealing in the material and things present, may be right. But much evidence, it seems to us, is present which points to unseen influences which could not be brought into court, as underlying the whole business. John Curry, mere lad of 14, and Wilbert Hess, 18, mere tools in the hands of cunning John Blymyer, anxious to see "witchcraft" at close range, have been set back a life-time! John Blymyer, according to the evidence, was the tool of some person or *spirit*, not brought into court. Who put the thought in the mind of Blymyer which he *could not blot out*, until life was extinct in Nelson D. Rehmeyer; until the latter's head, with many locks of hair, was buried six to eight feet under the ground?

"The murder has been solved", says the Commonwealth; (but has it the real murderers?); three young men will languish or thrive in the penitentiary, but there is a persistency of thought among any number of persons that there's a "nigger in the wood-pile" somewhere that hasn't been brought to the Bar of Justice!

"*Who* killed Nelson D. Rehmeyer?"

NAMES OF PERSONS CONNECTED WITH THE TRIAL

The names of York County Officials prominent in the trial are:

Presiding Judge—Hon. Ray P. Sherwood.
District Attorney—Amos W. Herrmann.
Counsel for the Defendant—Herbert W. Cohen.
Deputy Sheriff in charge of Prisoner—D. Wilson Kuehn.
Court Stenographer—Miss Grace Drayer.

The jurymen include the following persons (the figures preceding each name are the order of acceptance):

1. William E. Sprenkle, gentleman, 615 W. Market street, York.
6. Harry P. Kissinger, bookkeeper at York Trust Company, Springettsbury township.
8. H. K. Stauffer, gentleman, Spring Grove.
9. Noah A. Emig, farmer, Manheim township.
13. Curtis Leathery, farmer, Washington township.
14. Philip Myers, gentleman, Warrington township.
16. Charles R. McWilliams, wire worker, Hanover.
34. Walter Cunningham, painter, Springettsbury township.
35. Harry Warner, clerk, East Newton avenue, York.
36. Earl E. Brown, weaver, 327 Springdale avenue, York.
38. Charles Reisinger, loomfixer, 118 W. Jackson street, York.
44. John S. Fishel, justice of the peace, York Haven.

Forty-four talesmen were examined in the selection of the jury. The defense exercised 18 pre-emptory challenges and the Commonwealth six. There were nine challenges for cause allowed by the judge. Most of these were for the rejection of men who said that they had conscientious scruples against capital punishment or who had fixed opinions, which could not be changed by the evidence under oath in court.

The talesmen examined and rejected are Samuel Etter, Jerry Bupp, Wilbur Painter, John M. Esper, Samuel T. Sterner, James S. Fink, Levi Frey, Samuel T. Witmer, Raymond Oberdick, Edward D. Sterner, C. W. Myers, Chester Martin, William H. Saylor, Alexander E. McLean, C. E. Kessler, Lincoln McCurdy, B. Frank Gilbert, Percy J. Gnau, E. H. Hoffman, Raymond Hively, J. C. Hosler, Raymond L. Baustian, Harry Birnstock, Ralph W. Mitzel, H. B. Reisinger, Charles W. Myers, Charles M. Strickler, Wilson Barshinger, Robert Dietz, Emanuel Stover, Samuel C. Edgar, David E. Barshinger. Those rejected for cause were Messrs. Fink, Frey, Sterner, Gnau, Hoffman, Baustian, Charles W. Myers and William Barshinger.

THE GENESIS OF WITCHCRAFT.

The curious anachronism of witchcraft in 1929, reaching an apex of blood-chilling nyctophobia in the middle of a busy city next door to a bootlegger, arouses wonder.

The city of York, has received much unenviable publicity because of this strange situation, which resulted eventually in a brutal murder. The real facts, however, need not be considered as particularly disgraceful to York. True enough, the witchcraft superstition exists in that historic American community in a more aggravated form than the majority of its citizens are willing to admit. But this is not because the people of York are less cultured or more superstitious than those to be found in most other communities.

The vital point, seemingly overlooked during the recent trials, is not the fact that witchcraft practices exist, but the reason why they exist. The actual visible evidences are only superficial symptoms of a deep-seated trouble, brought to the surface by a peculiar combination of circumstances.

The fact is that there is incipient witchcraft everywhere. It is found in the hundreds of superstitions which prevail in all levels of society. In themselves they are innocent enough. Friday the thirteenth, knocking on wood, breaking mirrors, letting a baby see itself in a mirror, the three fluttering white butterflies prophetic of death, the danger of lighting three cigarets off one match, the recklessness of entering a house by one door and leaving by another—all these are familiar manifestations.

They do little harm in most communities. Few persons consider them very seriously. Only among the ignorant and child-minded, as a general rule, are they accepted without reservations.

Yet they are the essence of witchcraft. Only one step is necessary to transfer them into the grotesque superstition which produced such serious results in York. This step is the appearance of the charlatan.—Washington (D. C.,) *Star.*

IN PRAISE OF YORK, PA.

To the Editor of the N. Y. *World:*

"Little York" apparently is in for some front-page notoriety, if not advertising. Over where the "witches romp" isn't such a bad place, after all, although your readers could scarcely guess it from your news columns.

Seems to me I've read somewhere, and more than once, that the two richest agricultural counties in the whole United States, happen to be Lancaster and York, in Pennsylvania, apparently peopled 100 per cent. by ignoramuses and "hex" hounds, according to your reporter. Maybe he's right, but his reports and Uncle Sam's just somehow do not seem to jibe. Further, only a few months ago some prominent writer for the Saturday Evening *Post* dealt with the farm problem and began by suggesting that if Western farmers understood farming as do the men of Lancaster and York counties, there would be no national farm problem. Whether the disgruntled Westerners ought to learn how to "pow wow" or the lean hillbillies of York and Lancaster counties should get wise and unlearn farming, I can only guess. Further, if they really have weird signs on their barns and stables to scotch the "hex," as your reporter says, they also have just about the largest barns and stables and some of the fattest cattle and the largest finished market for steers east of Chicago. All this may go with ignorance, superstition, witchcraft and big bank balances, but as suggested it seems too unnatural and hurly-burly to ring true.

A town that sheltered the Revolutionary American Government for nearly a year; that produced Phineas Davis, who built at York some of the first locomotives bought by the Baltimore and Ohio Railroad; that for two generations supplied railway cars to all the young railroads of the country; that was the home of Judge Jeremiah Black, Attorney General of the United States and one of the most prominent lawyers of his time; a town that manufactures ice machines, safes and locks, water wheels, wall paper, silk, woven wire, steel chain and cable, agricultural machinery, cigars and what not, and was the residence of A. B. Farquhar, nationally known as publicist, writer and manufacturer—such a town, I think, can hardly be the same place your reporter was referring to, although his articles were dated there. Maybe it has changed for the worse since I saw it last. But everything is different these days! If your reporter is right it might be a good idea to import some of those Pennsylvania Dutch witch doctors and train them to "hex" the gunmen and gangsters around town. Then send more of them out West to settle Hoover's farm problem.   GEORGE I. KING.

Brooklyn, N. Y., *Jan.* 16.

THE STRANGEST MURDER TRIAL IN YEARS.

Editorial in the Philadelphia *Public Ledger.*

There is a quality of pathos as well as tragedy in the tale of the Witch Murder of York. The chief characters in the story—the dead "witch," the simple-minded souls who took his life, the families of those involved and the back-grounds of life disclosed—all have a strange look in this modern world. They seem somehow alien and afar off from everything in the life that moves around them.

Yet men who believe in "hexerai" and all the Powers of Darkness drive motor-cars through back roads to the house of the "witch." They turn from watching an airplane moving through the clouds to cast "spells" from the *Long Lost Friend*, that musty "witch-book" filled with tripled Latin crosses, holy words and black-typed "charms."

There is culture and high intelligence all around them in this very old town of York, that was old when the Revolution

[29]

was fought. It is the contrast between all this virile, modern, sound, vigorous and intelligent life and the dark mutterings of the "powwow men" and the "hill-hawks" that surround the case of three backward-minded countrymen with more than a passing interest.

The York County case is full of queer echoes out of a very old past. How old no one knows. White men brought "hexerai" to the hills, where it blended with the Indian "powwow." The dark shapes that moved in the minds of these hillmen and hillwomen, the ignorant "sorcery," the sordid "black magic" and the grotesque faith-healing go back for hundreds of years to medieval darkness.

These bedeviled and intangible things linger in the lonely spaces and in the mean streets. They come from even farther back than the Dark Ages. Some of them are undoubtedly "racial memories," tracing back to skin-clad men sitting around red fires glowing at the dark mouths of hillside caves.

It may be strange that the twilight of superstition should linger so long, but linger it does in a thousand places in America. When a screech owl whimpers in the trees outside, the mountaineer of the Great Smokies thrusts a shovel in the red hearth coals to drive the "witch bird" away.

Some of the gunmen of "Bloody Herrin" wore luck charms" around their hairy necks. The Ozark "hill-billy" believes that a silver bullet fired into a rude charcoal drawing of the witch is the only way to break the spell of witchcraft.

The *Long Lost Friend*, the "witchbook" of York, promises its owner that no evil shall befall him while it is in his possession. The warrior of Luzon clings to his "anting-anting" as some of the Indian fighters of the Old Frontier clung to their own strange "luck charms" to save them from bullet and tomahawk.

"Charms" are sold to this good day in great American cities. All the outworn superstition is not hidden in the back townships. The Pennsylvania hills are not the last and only strongholds of muddle-minded belief in "signs" and "spells" and bewitchments. For as Kipling sang a good many years ago:

> *Oh the road to En-Dor is the oldest road*
> *And the craziest road of all!*
> *Straight it runs to the Witch's abode,*
> *As it did in the days of Saul.* * * *

Human credulity is an amazing thing. Three country boys murdering a man in a lonely farmhouse to get a lock of his hair to break a "spell" is hardly more startling than that other tale of a "spirit message" from the dead Houdini. Belief in the supernatural dies hard, if it dies at all.

Contact with the world and such enlightenment as comes from education will spell the doom of the Powwow Man. The sorry figures and pathetic shapes of the trial at York are helping in their own sorry way to drive time-worn superstition back into its own dark past. They are unwilling instruments in breaking witchcraft's own devilish "spell" that grips the backward and simple mind.

The State owes these people something that is not being paid in the "witch trial." It owes them the kind of education that will make the "powwow" no more than a memory to the next generation.

———

The editor of the *Ledger* wrote well regarding the trial at York—and if only the various newspaper reporters would write as carefully as the editors, this "farce" would not have been so "serious."

The editor wrote carefully, and well, until his last paragraph, which we are sure he will not object to having his attention called to.

What kind of State does he think can make even the American people learn so much "that will make the "pow wow" (and other superstitions too numerous to mention) *no more than a memory to the next generation?"*

We have had thousands and thousands of years to overcome superstition; yet it loiters—it is a part of man's natural heritage—it cannot be avoided! The only "state" that can remove doubts and superstitions is the *State of Death!*

———

John Curry, the 14-year-old lad in the "witch" murder was sentenced to the penitentiary for life. The jury reached its verdict in an hour and three-quarters, after a trial lasting but a day.

Wilbert G. Hess, 18, was found guilty of murder in the second degree, and sentenced to from ten to twenty years in the penitentiary. The jury in this case reaching its verdict in about three hours.

Thus did York county arrange to take care of the three young "criminals," in trials that lasted just one week.

York county scarcely ever sends a man to death!

John George Hohman's

POW-WOWS; or LONG LOST FRIEND.

John George Hohman's

Pow-Wows;

OR,

Long Lost Friend.

A COLLECTION

OF MYSTERIOUS AND INVALUABLE

ARTS AND REMEDIES

FOR

MAN AS WELL AS ANIMALS.

WITH MANY PROOFS

*Of their virtue and efficacy in healing diseases, etc., the great-
er part of which was never published until they
appeared in print for the first time in
the U. S. in the year 1820.*

[REPRINTED FROM AN OLD EDITION]

☞ WHOEVER carries this book with him, is safe from all his enemies, visible or invisible; and whoever has this book with him cannot die without the holy corpse of Jesus Christ, nor drowned in any water, nor burn up in any fire, nor can any unjust sentence be passed upon him. So help me.

PUBLISHER'S HISTORICAL NOTE:

———

This edition of John George Hohman's *Pow-Wows; or Long Lost Friend* is reprinted entirely, word for word, from one of the many editions which have appeared in the English translations. The Westminster, Md., 1855, and Harrisburg, Pa., 1856, editions, are said to be the first English editions to appear on the book market. Since then thousands and thousands of cheaply printed and bound copies have been sold to a constantly buying public.

We recall the old adage: "Whatever is worth doing, is worth doing well;" hence the present remarkably well printed and bound copy is presented to the curious public. The folk-customs, manners, superstitions, beliefs and practices of a not so distant past, are, and always will be, subjects of interest to many, be they students, professional men and women, or they who still cling to these old-time Arts and Remedies.

Were it not for the past, the present would have nothing to depend on. Therefore, we are justified in the light of modern days, to show some outstanding practices of the past, by some said to be superstition—pure and simple; by others, a form of psychology, or misguided knowledge, or illusion.

While not paramount factors in everyday life of any particular class of people at the present time, nevertheless, many of the "remedies," and beliefs are in constant force and practice in the home and community life of untold numbers of people.

Many of the remedies included in the following pages may seem absurd to the average person of today, but when written, a hundred and ten years ago, most of them were "meat and drink" to our forbears. When,—(a hundred years from now)— the *truth* is written about the customs, fashions, beliefs and peculiarities of the American people of 1929, we will appear as strange, if not ludicrous to our coming generations, as the *sincere* beliefs and practices of our ancestors of a hundred years ago, appear to us today.

The use of manures for fertilization of our food stuffs

has always been an advantage, if not an absolute necessity; the more of it properly used, the better the harvest! Does mention of it in a book of this kind in connection with various remedies render an offensiveness to the one nostril— more so than does the other instance just mentioned, to the other nostril? Are critics always consistent?

We do not underwrite or endorse a single recipe in the following pages. Some of them, or all of them, may be good for something—or good for nothing! As stated previously, they are reprinted for what they may be worth — to the practitioner — as well as for the curious.

THE PUBLISHERS.

HARRISBURG, PA., *February* 1929.

PREFACE

TO THE FIRST EDITION OF THIS USEFUL BOOK.

———

The author would have preferred writing no preface whatever to this little book, were it not indispensably necessary, in order to meet the erroneous views some men entertain in regard to works of this character. The majority, undoubtedly, approve of the publication and sale of such books, yet some are always found who will persist in denouncing them as something wrong. This latter class I cannot help but pity, for being so far led astray; and I earnestly pray everyone who might find it in his power, to bring them from off their ways of error. It is true, whosoever taketh the name of JESUS in vain, committeth a great sin. Yet, is it not expressly written in the fiftieth Psalm, according to Luther's translation: "Call upon me in the day of trouble; I will deliver thee, and thou shalt glorify me." In the Catholic translation, the same passage is found in the forty-ninth Psalm, reading thus: "Call upon me in the day of thy trouble, and I will deliver thee, and thou shalt glorify me."

Where is the doctor who has ever cured or banished the panting or palpitation of the heart, and hideboundness? Where is the doctor who ever banished a wheal? Where is the doctor who ever banished the mother-fits? Where is the doctor that can cure mortification when it once seizes a member of the body? All these cures, and a great many more mysterious and wonderful things are contained in this book; and its author could take an oath at any time upon the fact of his having successfully applied many of the prescriptions contained herein.

I say: any and every man who knowingly neglects using this book in saving the eye, or the leg, or any other limb of his fellow-man, is guilty of the loss of such limb, and thus commits a sin, by which he may forfeit to himself all hope of salvation. Such men refuse to call upon the Lord in their trouble, although He especially commands it. If men were not allowed to use sympathetic words, nor the name of the MOST HIGH, it certainly would not have been revealed to them; and what is more, the Lord would not help where they are made use of. God can in no manner be forced to intercede where it is not his divine pleasure.

Another thing I have to notice here: There are men who will say, if one has used sympathetic words in vain, the medicines of doctors could not avail any, because the words did not affect a cure. This is only the excuse of physicians; because whatever cannot be cured by sympathetic words, can much less be cured by any doctor's craft or cunning. I could name at any time that Catholic priest whose horse was cured with mere words; and I could also give the name of the man who did it. I knew the priest well; he formerly resided in Westmoreland county. If it was desired, I could also name a Reformed preacher who cured several persons of the fever, merely by writing them some tickets for that purpose; and even the names of those persons I could mention. This preacher formerly resided in Berks county. If men but use out of this book what they actually need, they surely commit no sin; yet woe unto those who are guilty that anyone loses his life in consequence of mortification, or loses a limb, or the sight of the eye! Woe unto those who misconstrue these things at the moment of danger, or who follow the ill advice of any preacher who might teach them not to mind what the Lord says in the fiftieth Psalm. "Call upon me in the day of trouble: I will deliver thee, and thou shalt glorify me." Woe unto those who, in obeying the directions of a preacher, neglect using any means offered by this book against mortification, or inflammation, or the wheal. I am willing to follow the preacher in all reasonable things, yet when I am in danger and he advises me not to use any prescriptions found in this book, in such a case I shall not obey him. And woe also unto those who use the name of the Lord in vain and for trifling purposes.

I have given many proofs of the usefulness of this book, and I could yet do it at any time. I sell my books publicly, and not secretly, as other mystical books are sold. I am willing that my books should be seen by everybody, and I shall not secrete or hide myself from any preacher. I, Hohman, too, have some knowledge of the Scriptures, and I know when to pray and call unto the Lord for assistance. The publication of books (provided they are useful and morally right) is not prohibited in the United States, as is the case in other countries where kings and despots hold tyrannical sway over the people. I place myself upon the broad platform of the liberty of the press and of conscience, in regard to this useful book, and it shall ever be my most heartfelt desire that all men might have an opportunity of using it to their good, in the name of Jesus.

Given at Rosenthal, near Reading, Berks county, Penn., on the 31st day of July, in the year of our Lord, 1819.

JOHN GEORGE HOHMAN.
Author and original publisher of this book.

TESTIMONIALS,

Which go to show at any time, that I, Hohman, have successfully applied the prescriptions of this book.

BENJAMIN STOUDT, the son of a Lutheran schoolmaster, at Reading, suffered dreadfully from a wheal in the eye. In a little more than 24 hours this eye was as sound as the other one, by the aid I rendered him with the help of God, in the year 1817.

HENRY JORGER, residing in Reading, brought to me a boy who suffered extreme pain, caused by a wheal in the eye, in the year 1814. In a little more than 24 hours, I, with the help of God, have healed him.

JOHN BAYER, son of Jacob Bayer, now living near Reading, had an ulcer on his leg, which gave him great pain. I attended him, and in a short time the leg was well. This was in the year 1818.

LANDLIN GOTTWALD, formerly residing in Reading, had a severe pain in his one arm. In about 24 hours I cured his arm.

CATHARINE MECK, at that time in Alsace township, suffered very much from a wheal in the eye. In a little more than 24 hours the eye was healed.

MR. SILVIS, of Reading, came to my house while engaged at the brewery of my neighbor. He felt great pain in the eye caused by a wheal. I cured his eye in a little more than 24 hours.

ANNA SNYDER, of Alsace township, had a severe pain in one of her fingers. In a little more than twenty-four hours she felt relieved.

MICHAEL HARTMAN, JR., living in Alsace township, had a child with a very sore mouth. I attended it and in a little more than twenty-four hours it was well again.

JOHN BINGEMANN, at Ruscombmanor, Berks county, had a boy who burnt himself dreadfully. My wife came to that place in the fall of the year 1812. Mortification had already set in—my wife had sympathy for it, and in a short time the mortification was banished. The boy was soon after perfectly cured and became well again. It was about the same time my wife cured John Bingemann's wife of the wild-fire, which she had on a sore leg.

SUSANNA GOMBER had a severe pain in the head. In a short time I relieved her.

The wife of David Brecht also felt a severe pain in the head, and was relieved by me in a short time.

JOHN JUNKINS' daughter and daughter-in-law both suffered very much from pain in the head; and his wife too had a sore cheek, on which the wild-fire had broken out severely. The headache of the daughter and the daughter-in-law was banished by me; and the wild-fire of the wife was cured in some seven or nine hours; the swelled cheek burst open and healed very fast. The woman had been laid up several days already on account of it. The family of Junkins live at Nackenmixen, but Brecht and Gomber reside in and near Reading. Nackenmixen is in Bucks county. The four last mentioned were cured in the year 1819.

The daughter of John Arnold scalded herself with boiling coffee; the handle of the pot broke off while she was pouring out coffee, and the coffee ran over the arm and burnt it severely. I was present and witnessed the accident. I banished the burning; the arm did not get sore at all, and healed in a short time. This was in the year 1815. Mr. Arnold lived near Lebanon, Lebanon county, Penn.

JACOB STOUEFER, at Heckak, Bucks county, had a little child who was subject to convulsions every hour. I sold him a book containing the 25 letters; and he was persuaded by his neighbor, Henry Frankenfield, to try these 25 letters. The result was that the child was instantaneously free from convulsions and perfectly well. These letters are also to be found in this book.

☞If any one of the above named witnesses, who have been cured by me and my wife through the help of God, dares to call me a liar, and deny having been relieved by us, although they have confessed that they have been cured by us, I shall, if it is at all possible, compel them to repeat their confession before a Justice of the Peace.

A letter to cure rheumatism, sold at from one to two dollars, and did not even give directions how to make use of it; these depending on verbal communications. John Allgaier, of Reading, had a very sore finger. I used sympathy to banish the wild-fire and to cure the finger. The very next morning the wild-fire was gone; he scarcely felt any pain, and the finger began to heal very fast. This was in 1819.

☞ This book is partly derived from a work published by a Gypsy, and partly from secret writings, and collected with much pain and trouble, from all parts of the world, at different periods, by the author, John George Hohman. I did not wish to publish it; my wife, also was opposed to its publication; but my compassion for my suffering fellow-men was too strong, for I had seen many a one lose his entire sight by a wheal, and his life or limb by mortification. And how dreadfully has many a woman suffered from mother-fits? And I therefore ask thee again, oh friend, male or female, is it not to my everlasting praise, that I have had such books printed? Do I not deserve the rewards of God for it? Where else is the physician that could cure these diseases? Besides that I am a poor man in needy circumstances, and it is a help to me if I can make a little money with the sale of my books.

The Lord bless the beginning and the end of this little work, and be with us, that we may not misuse it, and thus commit a heavy sin! The word *misuse* means as much as to use it for anything unnecessary. God bless us! Amen. The word *Amen* means as much as that the Lord might bring to pass in reality what had been asked for in prayer.

HOHMAN.

NOTE.

There are many in America who believe neither in a hell nor in a heaven; but in Germany there are not so many of these persons found. I, Hohman, ask: Who can immediately banish the wheal, or mortification? I reply, and I, Hohman, say: All this is done by the Lord. Therefore, a hell and a heaven must exist; and I think very little of any one who dares deny it.

JOHN GEORGE HOHMAN'S POW-WOWS

ON

ARTS AND REMEDIES.

A good Remedy for Hysterics (or Mother Fits), to be used three times.—Put that joint of the thumb which sits in the palm of the hand on the bare skin covering the small bone which stands out above the pit of the heart, and speak the following at the same time:

Matrix, patrix, lay thyself right and safe,
Or thou or I shall on the third day fill the grave. † † †

Another Remedy for Hysterics and for Colds.—This must be attened to every evening, that is, whenever you pull off your shoes and stockings, run your finger in between all the toes and smell it. This will certainly effect a cure.

A certain Remedy to stop Bleeding, which cures, no matter how far a person be away, if only his first name is rightly pronounced while using it:

Jesus Christ, dearest blood!
That stoppeth the pain and stoppeth the blood.
In this help you [*first name*] God the Father, God the Son, God the Holy Ghost. Amen.

A remedy to be used when anyone is falling away, and which has cured many persons.—Let the person in perfect soberness and without having conversed with anyone, catch rain in a pot, before sunrise; boil an egg in this; bore three small holes in this egg with a needle, and carry it to an ant-hill made by big ants; and the person will feel relieved as soon as the egg is devoured.

Another Remedy to be applied when anyone is sick, which has effected many a cure where doctors could not help.—Let the sick person, without having conversed with anyone, put water in a bottle before sunrise, close it up tight, and put it immediately in some box or chest, lock it and stop up the keyhole; the key must be carried in one of the pockets for three days, as nobody dare have it except the person who puts the bottle with water in the chest or box.

A good Remedy for Worms, to be used for men as well as for Cattle:

> Mary, God's mother, traversed the land,
> Holding three worms close in her hand;
> One was white, the other was black, the third was red.

This must be repeated three times, at the same time stroking the person or animal with the hand; and at the end of each application strike the back of the person or the animal, to wit: at the first application once, at the second application twice, and at the third application three times; and then set the worms a certain time, but not less than three minutes.

A good Remedy against Calumniation or Slander.—If you are calumniated or slandered to your very skin, to your very flesh, to your very bones, cast it back upon the false tongues.

† † †

Take off your shirt, and turn it wrong side out, and then run your two thumbs along your body, close under the ribs, starting at the pit of the heart down to the thighs.

A good Remedy for the Colic.—I warn ye, ye colic fiends! There is one sitting in judgment, who speaketh: just or unjust. Therefore beware, ye colic fiends!   † † †

A good Remedy for the Fever. — Good morning, dear Thursday! Take away from [*name*] the 77-fold fevers. Oh! thou dear Lord Jesus Christ, take them away from him!

† † †

This must be used on Thursday for the first time, on Friday for the second time, and on Saturday for the third time; and each time thrice. The prayer of faith has also to be said each time, and not a word dare be spoken to anyone until the sun has risen. Neither dare the sick person speak to anyone till after sunrise; nor eat pork, nor drink milk, nor cross a running water, for nine days.

To Attach a Dog to a Person, Provided Nothing Else was Used Before to Effect it.—Try to draw some of your blood, and let the dog eat it along with his food, and he will stay with you. Or scrape the four corners of your table while you are eating, and continue to eat with the same knife after having scraped the corners of the table. Let the dog eat those scrapings, and he will stay with you.

A very good Remedy for Palpitation of the Heart, and for Persons who are Hide-Bound:

Palpitation and hide-bound, be off [*name*] ribs,
Since Christ, our Lord, spoke truth with his lips.

A Precaution against Injuries.—Whoever carries the right eye of a wolf fastened inside of his right sleeve, remains free from all injuries.

To make a Wand for Searching for Iron, Ore or Water.—On the first night of Christmas, between 11 and 12 o'clock, break off from any tree a young twig of one year's growth, in the three highest names (Father, Son and Holy Ghost), at the same time facing toward sunrise. Whenever you apply this wand in searching for anything, apply it three times. The twig must be forked, and each end of the fork must be held in one hand, so that the third and thickest part of it stands up, but do not hold it too tight. Strike the ground with the thickest end, and that which you desire will appear immediately, if there is any in the ground where you strike. The words to be spoken when the wand is thus applied are as follows:

Archangel Gabriel, I conjure thee in the name of God, the Almighty, to tell me, is there any water here or not? do tell me!   † † †

If you are searching for Iron or Ore, you have to say the same, only mention the name of what you are searching for.

How to Obtain Things which are Desired.—If you call upon another to ask for a favor, take care to carry a little of the five-finger grass with you, and you shall certainly obtain that you desired.

A Sure Way of Catching Fish.—Take rose seed and mustard seed, and the foot of a weasel, and hang these in a net, and the fish will certainly collect there.

A safe Remedy for various Ulcers, Boils and other Defects.—Take the root of an iron-weed, and tie it around the neck; it cures running ulcers; it also serves against obstructions in the bladder (stranguary), and cures the piles, if the roots are boiled in water with honey, and drank; it cleans and heals the lungs and effects a good breath. If this root is planted among grape vines or fruit trees, it promotes the growth very much. Children who carry it are educated without any difficulty; they become fond of all useful arts and sciences, and grow up joyfully and cheerfully.

GOOD REMEDY FOR MORTIFICATION AND INFLAMMATION

Sanctus Itorius res, call the rest. Here the mother of God came to his assistance, reaching out her snow-white hand, against the hot and cold brand.   † † †

Make three crosses with the thumb. Everything which is applied in words, must be applied three times, and an interval of several hours must intervene each time, and for the third time it is to be applied the next day, unless where it is otherwise directed.

TO PREVENT WICKED OR MALICIOUS PERSONS FROM DOING YOU AN INJURY—AGAINST WHOM IT IS OF GREAT POWER

Dullix, ix, ux. Yea, you can't come over Pontio; Pontio is above Pilato.   † † †

A VERY GOOD REMEDY TO DESTROY BOTS OR WORMS IN HORSES

You must mention the name of the horse, and say: "If you have any worms, I will catch you by the forehead. If they be white, brown or red, they shall and must now all be dead." You must shake the head of the horse three times, and pass your hand over his back three times to and fro.   † † †

TO CURE THE POLL-EVIL IN HORSES, IN TWO OR THREE APPLICATIONS.

Break off three twigs from a cherry-tree: one towards morning, one towards evening, and one towards midnight. Cut three small pieces off the hind part of your shirt, and wrap each of those twigs in one of these pieces; then clean the poll-evil with the twigs and leave them under the eaves. The ends of the twigs which had been in the wound must be turned toward the north; after which you must do your business on them, that is to say, you must dirty them; then cover it, leaving the rags around the twigs. After all this the wound must be again stirred with the three twigs, in one or two days, and the twigs placed as before.

A GOOD REMEDY FOR BAD WOUNDS AND BURNS.

The word of God, the milk of Jesus' mother, and Christ's blood, is for all wounds and burnings good.   † † †

It is the safest way in all these cases to make the crosses with the hand or thumb three times over the affected parts; that is to say, over all those things to which the three crosses are attached.

A VERY GOOD REMEDY FOR THE WILD-FIRE.

Wild-fire and the dragon, flew over a wagon,
The wild-fire abated and the dragon skated.

TO STOP PAINS OR SMARTING IN A WOUND.

Cut three small twigs from a tree—each to be cut off in
one cut—rub one end of each twig in the wound, and wrap
them separately in a piece of white paper, and put them in
a warm and dry place.

TO DESTROY WARTS.

Roast chicken-feet and rub the warts with them; then
bury them under the eaves.

TO BANISH THE WHOOPING COUGH.

Cut three small bunches of hair from the crown of the
head of a child that has never seen its father; sew this hair
up in an unbleached rag and hang it around the neck of
the child having the whooping cough. The thread with which
the rag is sewed must also be unbleached.

ANOTHER REMEDY FOR THE WHOOPING COUGH WHICH HAS CURED THE MAJORITY OF THOSE WHO HAVE APPLIED IT.

Thrust the child having the whooping cough three times
through a blackberry bush, without speaking or saying anything. The bush, however, must be grown fast at two ends,
and the child must be thrust through three times in the same
manner, that is to say, from the same side it was thrust
through in the first place.

A GOOD REMEDY TO STOP BLEEDING.

This is the day on which the injury happened. Blood, thou
must stop, until the Virgin Mary bring forth another son.
Repeat these words three times.

A GOOD REMEDY FOR THE TOOTHACHE.

Stir the sore tooth with a needle until it draws blood; then
take a thread and soak it with this blood. Then take vinegar and flour, mix them well so as to form a paste and spread
it on a rag, then wrap this rag around the root of an apple-
tree, and tie it very close with the above thread, after which
the root must be well covered with ground.

HOW TO WALK AND STEP SECURELY IN ALL PLACES.

Jesus walketh with [name]. He is my head; I am his
limb. Therefore walketh Jesus with [name].   † † †

A VERY GOOD REMEDY FOR THE COLIC.

Take half a gill of good rye whiskey, and a pipe full of tobacco; put the whiskey in a bottle, then smoke the tobacco and blow the smoke into the bottle, shake it well and drink it. This has cured the author of this book and many others. Or, take a white clay pipe which has turned blackish from smoking, pound it to a fine powder, and take it. This will have the same effect.

TO BANISH CONVULSIVE FEVERS

Write the following letters on a piece of white paper, sew it on a piece of linen or muslin, and hang it around the neck until the fever leaves you:

```
A b a x a C a t a b a x a
A b a x a C a t a b a x
A b a x a C a t a b a
A b a x a C a t a b
A b a x a C a t a
A b a x a C a t
A b a x a C a
A b a x a C
A b a x a
A b a x
A b a
A b
A
```

HOW TO BANISH THE FEVER

Write the following words upon a paper and wrap it up in knot-grass, *(breiten Megrieh,)* and then tie it upon the body of the person who has the fever:

> *Potmat sineat,*
> *Potmat sineat,*
> *Potmat sineat.*

A VERY GOOD PLASTER

I doubt very much whether any physician in the United States can make a plaster equal to this. It heals the white swelling, and has cured the sore leg of a woman who for eighteen years had used the prescriptions of doctors in vain.

Take two quarts of cider, one pound of bees'-wax, one pound of sheep-tallow, and one pound of tobacco; boil the tobacco in the cider till the strength is out, and then strain it, and add the other articles to the liquid; stir it over a gentle fire till all is dissolved.

TO MAKE A GOOD EYE-WATER

Take four cents' worth of white vitriol, four cents' worth of prepared spicewort (calamus root), four cents' worth of cloves, a gill of good whiskey and a gill of water. Make the calamus fine and mix all together; then use it after it has stood a few hours.

A VERY GOOD REMEDY FOR THE WHITE SWELLING

Take a quart of unslacked lime, and pour two parts of water on it; stir it well and let it stand over night. The scum that collects on the lime-water must be taken off, and a pint of flax-seed oil poured in, after which it must be stirred until it becomes somewhat consistent; then put it in a pot or pan, and add a little lard and wax; melt it well, and make a plaster, and apply it to the parts affected —the plaster should be renewed every day, or at least every other day, until the swelling is gone.

A REMEDY FOR EPILEPSY, PROVIDED THE SUBJECT HAD NEVER FALLEN INTO FIRE OR WATER

Write reversedly or backwards upon a piece of paper: "IT IS ALL OVER!" This is to be written but once upon the paper; then put it in a scarlet-red cloth, and then wrap it in a piece of unbleached linen, and hang it around the neck on the first Friday of the new moon. The thread with which it is tied must also be unbleached.   † † †

REMEDY FOR BURNS

"Blow, I blow on thee!"—It must be blown on three times in the same breath, like the fire by the sun.   † † †

TO STOP BLEEDING

Count backwards from fifty inclusive till you come down to three. As soon as you arrive at three, you will be done bleeding.

A REMEDY TO RELIEVE PAIN

Take a rag which was tied over a wound for the first time, and put it in water together with some copperas; but do not venture to stir the copperas until you are certain of the pain having left you.

A GOOD REMEDY FOR THE TOOTHACHE

Cut out a piece of greensward (sod) in the morning before sunrise, quite unbeshrewdly from any place, breathe three times upon it, and put it down upon the same place from which it was taken.

TO REMOVE BRUISES AND PAINS

Bruise, that shalt not heat;
Bruise, thou shalt not sweat;
Bruise, thou shalt not run,
No more than Virgin Mary shall bring forth
another son.   † † †

A REMARKABLE PASSAGE FROM THE BOOK OF ALBERTUS MAGNUS

It says: If you burn a large frog to ashes, and mix the aches with water, you will obtain an ointment that will, if put on any place covered with hair, destroy the hair and prevent it from growing again.

ANOTHER PASSAGE FROM THE WORK OF ALBERTUS MAGNUS.

If you find the stone which a vulture has in his knees, and which you may find by looking sharp, and put it in the victuals of two persons who hate each other, it causes them to make up and be good friends.

TO CURE FITS OR CONVULSIONS

You must go upon another person's land, and repeat the following words: "I go before another court—I tie up my 77-fold fits." Then cut three small twigs off any tree on the land; in each twig you must make a knot. This must be done on a Friday morning before sunrise, in the decrease of the moon unbeshrewdly. † † † Then over your body where you feel the fits you make the crosses. And thus they may be made in all cases where they are applied.

CURE FOR THE HEADACHE

Tame thou flesh and bone, like Christ in Paradise; and who will assist thee, this I tell thee [*name*] for your repentance sake. † † † This you must say three times, each time lasting for three minutes, and your headache will soon cease. But if your headache is caused by strong drink, or otherwise will not leave you soon, then you must repeat those words every minute. This, however, is not often necessary in regard to headache.

TO MEND BROKEN GLASS

Take common cheese and wash it well, unslaked lime and the white of eggs, rub all these well together until it becomes one mass, and then use. If it is made right, it will certainly hold.

HOW TO MAKE CATTLE RETURN TO THE SAME PLACE

Pull out three small bunches of hair, one between the horns, one from the middle of the back, and one near the tail, and make your cattle eat it in their feed.

ANOTHER METHOD OF MAKING CATTLE RETURN HOME

Take a handful of salt, go upon your fields and make your cattle walk three times around the same stump or stone, each time keeping the same direction; that is to say, you must three times arrive at the same end of the stump or stone at which you started from, and then let your cattle lick the salt from the stump or stone.

TO PREVENT THE HESSIAN FLY FROM INJURING THE WHEAT

Take pulverized charcoal, make ley of it, and soak the seed wheat in it; take it out of the ley, and on every bushel of wheat sprinkle a quart of urine; stir it well, then spread it out to dry.

TO PREVENT CHERRIES FROM RIPENING BEFORE MARTINMAS

Engraft the twigs upon a mulberry-tree, and your desire is accomplished.

STINGING NETTLES—GOOD FOR BANISHING FEARS AND FANCIES, AND TO CAUSE FISH TO COLLECT

Whenever you hold this weed in your hand together with Millifolia, you are safe from all fears and fancies that frequently deceive men. If you mix it with a decoction of the hemlock, and rub your hands with it, and put the rest in water that contains fish, you will find the fish to collect around your hands. Whenever you pull your hands out of the water, the fish disappear by returning to their former places.

HELIOTROPE (SUN-FLOWER) A MEANS TO PREVENT CALUMNIATION.

The virtues of this plant are miraculous. If it be collected in the sign of the lion, in the month of August, and wrapped up in a laurel leaf together with the tooth of a wolf. Whoever carries this about him, will never be addressed harshly by anyone, but all will speak to him kindly and peaceably. And if anything has been stolen from you put this under your head during the night, and you will surely see the whole figure of the thief. This has been found true.

TO HEAL A SORE MOUTH

If you have the scurvy, or quinsy too,
I breathe my breath three times into you,

† † †

A GOOD REMEDY FOR CONSUMPTION

Consumption, I order thee out of the bones into the flesh, out of the flesh upon the skin, out of the skin into the wilds of the forest.   † † †

SWALLOW-WORT

A means to overcome and end all fighting and anger, and to cause a sick man to weep when his health is restored, or to sing with a cheerful voice when on his death bed; also a very good remedy for dim eyes or shining of the eyes. This weed grows at the time when the swallows build their nests or eagles breed. If a man carries this about him, together with the heart of a mole, he shall overcome all fighting and anger. If these things are put upon the head of a sick man, he shall weep at the restoration of his health, and sing with a cheerful voice when he comes to die. When the swallow-wort blooms, the flowers must be pounded up and boiled, and then the water must be poured off into another vessel, and again be placed to the fire and carefully skimmed; then it must be filtered through a cloth and preserved, and whosoever has dim eyes or shining eyes, may bathe his eyes with it, and they will become clear and sound.

FOR THE HOLLOW HORN IN COWS.

Bore a small hole in the hollow horn, milk the same cow, and squirt her milk into the horn; this is the best cure. Use a syringe to squirt the milk into the horn.

A VERY GOOD AND CERTAIN MEANS OF DESTROYING THE WHEAL IN THE EYE.

Take a dirty plate; if you have none, you can easily dirty one, and the person for whom you are using sympathy shall in a few minutes find the pain much relieved. You must hold that side of the plate or dish, which is used in eating, toward the eye. While you hold the plate before the eye, you must say:

Dirty plate, I press thee,
Wheal in the eye, do flee.
† † †

TO MAKE CHICKENS LAY MANY EGGS.

Take the dung of rabbits, pound it to powder, mix it with bran, wet the mixture till it forms lumps, and feed your chickens with it, and they will keep on laying a great many eggs.

WORDS TO BE SPOKEN WHILE MAKING DIVINATORY WANDS.

In making divinatory wands, they must be broken as before directed, and while breaking and before using them, the following words must be spoken:

Divining rod, do thou keep that power,
Which God gave unto thee at the very first hour.

HOW TO DESTROY A TAPE-WORM.

Worm, I conjure thee by the living God, that thou shalt flee this blood and this flesh, like as God the Lord will shun that judge who judges unjustly, although he might have judged aright. † † †

A GOOD REMEDY FOR BOTS IN HORSES.

Every time you use this, you must stroke the horse down with the hand three times, and lead it about three times holding its head toward the sun, saying: "The Holy One saith: Joseph passed over a field and there he found three small worms; the one being black, another being brown, and the third being red; thou shalt die and be dead."

HOW TO CURE A BURN.

Three holy men went out walking,
They did bless the heat and the burning;
They blessed that it might not increase;
They blessed that it might quickly cease!
† † †

TO CURE THE BITE OF A SNAKE.

God has created all things and they were good;
Thou only, serpent, art damned,
Cursed be thou and thy sting.
† † †
Zing, zing, zing!

SECURITY AGAINST MAD DOGS.

Dog, hold thy nose to the ground,
God has made me and thee, hound!
† † †

This you must repeat in the direction of the dog; and the three crosses you must make toward the dog, and the words must be spoken before he sees you.

TO REMOVE PAIN AND HEAL UP WOUNDS WITH THREE SWITCHES.

With this switch and Christ's dear blood,
I banish your pain and do you good!
† † †

Mind it well: you must in one cut, sever from a tree, a young branch pointing toward sunrise, and then make three pieces of it, which you successively put in the wound. Holding them in your hand, you take the one toward your right side first. Everything prescribed in this book must be used three times, even if the three crosses should not be affixed.

Words are always to have an interval of half an hour, and between the second and third time should pass a whole night, except where it is otherwise directed. The above three sticks, after the end of each has been put into the wound as before directed, must be put in a piece of white paper, and placed where they will be warm and dry.

REMEDY FOR FEVER, WORMS, AND THE COLIC.

Jerusalem, thou Jewish city,
In which Christ our Lord, was born,
Thou shalt turn into water and blood,
Because it is for [*name*] fever, worms, and colic good.

HOW TO CURE WEAKNESS OF THE LIMBS.

Take the buds of the birch tree, or the inner bark of the root of the tree at the time of the budding of the birch, and make a tea of it, and drink it occasionally through the day. Yet, after having used it for two weeks, it must be discontinued for a while, before it is resorted to again; and during the two weeks of its use it is well at times to use water for a day instead of the tea.

ANOTHER REMEDY FOR WEAKNESS.

Take Bittany and St. John's wort, and put them in good old rye whiskey. To drink some of this in the morning before having taken anything else, is very wholesome and good. A tea made of the acorns of the white oak is very good for weakness of the limbs.

TO MAKE HORSES THAT REFUSE THEIR FEED TO EAT AGAIN— ESPECIALLY APPLICABLE WHEN THEY ARE AFFLICTED IN THIS MANNER ON THE PUBLIC ROADS.

Open the jaws of the horse, which refuses his feed, and knock three times on his palate. This will certainly cause the horse to eat again without hesitation and to go along willingly.

A GOOD METHOD OF DESTROYING RATS AND MICE.

Every time you bring grain into your barn, you must, in putting down the three first sheaves, repeat the following words: "Rats and mice, these three sheaves I give to you, in order that you may not destroy any of my wheat." The name of the kind of grain must also be mentioned.

TO CURE ANY EXCRESCENCE OR WEN ON A HORSE.

Take any bone which you accidentally find, for you dare not be looking for it, and rub the wen of the horse with it, always bearing in mind that it must be done in the decreasing moon, and the wen will certainly disappear. The bone, however, must be replaced as it was lying before.

HOW TO PREPARE A GOOD EYE-WATER.

Take one cunce of white vitriol and one ounce of sugar of lead, dissolve them in oil of rosemary, and put it in a quart bottle, which you fill up with rose-water. Bathe the eyes with it night and morning.

HOW TO CAUSE MALE OR FEMALE THIEVES TO STAND STILL, WITHOUT BEING ABLE TO MOVE BACKWARD OR FORWARD.

In using any prescriptions of this book in regard to making others stand still, it is best to be walking about; and repeat the following three times:

"Oh Peter, oh Peter, borrow the power from God; what I shall bind with the bands of a Christian hand, shall be bound; all male and female thieves, be they great or small, young or old, shall be spell-bound, by the power of God, and not be abe to walk forward or backward until I see them with my eyes, and give them leave with my tongue, except it be that they count for me all the stones that may be between heaven and earth, all rain-drops, all the leaves and all the grasses in the world. This I pray for the repentance of my enemies."   † † †

Repeat your articles of faith and the Lord's Prayer.

If the thieves are to remain alive, the sun dare not shine upon them before their release. There are two ways of releasing them, which will be particularly stated: The first is this, that you tell them, in the name of St. John, to leave; the other is as follows: "The words which have bound thee shall give thee free."   † † †

TO CURE THE SWEENEY IN HORSES.

Take a piece of old bacon, and cut it into small pieces, put them in a pan and roast them well, put a handful of fish-worms, a gill of oats and three spoonfuls of salt into it; roast the whole of this until it turns black, and then filter it through a cloth; after which you put a gill of soft soap, half a gill of rye whiskey, half a gill of vinegar, and half a pint of rain-water to it; mix it well, and smear it over the part affected with sweeney on the third, sixth, and the ninth day of the new moon, and warm it with an oaken board.

HOW TO MAKE MOLASSES.

Take pumpkins, boil them, press the juice out of them, and boil the juice to a proper consistence. There is nothing else necessary. The author of this book, John George Hohman, has tasted this molasses, thinking it was the genuine kind, until the people of the house told him what it was.

TO MAKE GOOD BEER.

Take a handful of hops, five or six gallons of water, about three tablespoonfuls of ginger, half a gallon of molasses; filter the water, hops and ginger into a tub containing the molasses.

CURE FOR THE EPILEPSY.

Take a turtle dove, cut its throat, and let the person afflicted with epilepsy, drink the blood.

ANOTHER WAY TO MAKE CATTLE RETURN HOME.

Feed your cattle out of a pot or kettle used in preparing your dinner, and they will always return to your stable.

A VERY GOOD REMEDY TO CURE SORES.

Boil the bulbs (roots) of the white lily in cream, and put it on the sore in the form of a plaster. Southern-wort has the same effect.

A GOOD CURE FOR WOUNDS.

Take the bones of a calf, and burn them until they turn to powder, and then strew it into the wound. The powder prevents the flesh from putrefying, and is therefore of great importance in healing the wound.

TO MAKE AN OIL OUT OF PAPER, WHICH IS GOOD FOR SORE EYES.

A man from Germany informed me that to burn two sheets of white paper would produce about three drops of oil or water, which would heal all sores in or about the eye if rubbed with it. Any affection of the eyes can be cured in this way, as long as the apple of the eye is sound.

TO DESTROY CRAB-LICE.

Take capuchin powder, mix it with hog's lard, and smear yourself with it. Or boil cammock, and wash the place where the lice keep themselves.

TO PREVENT THE WORST KIND OF PAPER FROM BLOTTING.

Dissolve alum in water, and put it on the paper, and I, Hohman, would like to see who cannot write on it, when it is dried.

A VERY GOOD REMEDY FOR THE GRAVEL.

The author of this book, John George Hohman, applied this remedy, and soon felt relieved. I knew a man who could find no relief from the medicine of any doctor; he then used the following remedy, to wit: he ate every morning seven peach-stones before tasting anything else, which relieved him very much; but as he had the gravel very bad, he was obliged to use it constantly. I, Hohman, have used it for several weeks. I still feel a touch of it now and then, yet I had it so badly that I cried out aloud every time that I had to make water. I owe a thousand thanks to God and the person who told me of this remedy.

A GOOD REMEDY FOR THOSE WHO CANNOT KEEP THEIR WATER.

Burn a hog's bladder to powder, and take it inwardly.

TO REMOVE A WEN DURING THE CRESCENT MOON.

Look over the wen, directly towards the moon, and say "Whatever grows, does grow; and whatever diminishes, does diminish." This must be said three times in the same breath.

TO DESTROY FIELD-MICE AND MOLES.

Put unslacked lime in their holes and they will disappear.

TO REMOVE A SCUM OR SKIN FROM THE EYE.

Before sunrise on St. Bartholomew's Day, you must dig up four or five roots of the dandelion weed, taking good care to get the ends of the roots; then you must procure a rag and a thread that have never been in the water; the thread, which dare not have a single knot in it, is used in sewing up the roots into the rag, and the whole is then to be hung before the eye until the scum disappears. The tape by which it is fastened must never have been in the water.

FOR DEAFNESS, ROARING OR BUZZING IN THE EAR, AND FOR TOOTHACHE.

A few drops of refined camphor-oil put upon cotton, and thus applied to the aching tooth, relieves very much. When put in the ear it strengthens the hearing and removes the roaring and whizzing in the same.

A GOOD WAY TO CAUSE CHILDREN TO CUT THEIR TEETH WITHOUT PAIN.

Boil the brain of a rabbit and rub the gums of the children with it, and their teeth will grow without pain to them.

FOR VOMITING AND DIARRHŒA.

Take pulverized cloves and eat them together with bread soaked in red wine, and you will soon find relief. The cloves may be put upon the bread.

TO HEAL BURNS.

Pound or press the juice of male fern, and put it on the burnt spots and they will heal very fast. Better yet, however, if you smear the above juice upon a rag, and put it on like a plaster.

A VERY GOOD CURE FOR WEAKNESS OF THE LIMBS, FOR THE PURIFICATION OF THE BLOOD, FOR THE INVIGORATION OF THE HEAD AND HEART, AND TO REMOVE GIDDINESS, ETC.

Take two drops of oil of cloves in a tablespoonful of white wine early in the morning, and before eating anything else. This is also good for the mother-pains and the colic. The oil of cloves which you buy in the drug stores will answer the purpose. These remedies are also applicable to cure the cold when it settles in the bowels, and to stop vomiting. A few drops of this oil poured upon cotton and applied to the aching teeth, relieves the pain.

FOR DYSENTERY AND DIARRHŒA.

Take the moss off of trees, and boil it in red wine, and let those who are affected with those diseases drink it.

CURE FOR THE TOOTHACHE.

Hohman, the author of this book, has cured the severest toothache more than sixty times, with this remedy, and, out of the sixty times he applied it, it failed but once in effecting a cure. Take blue vitriol and put a piece of it in the hollow tooth, yet not too much; spit out the water that collects in the mouth, and be careful to swallow none. I do not know whether it is good for teeth that are not hollow, but I should judge it would cure any kind of toothache.

ADVICE TO PREGNANT WOMEN.

Pregnant women must be very careful not to use any camphor; and no camphor should be administered to those women who have the mother-fits.

CURE FOR THE BITE OF A MAD DOG.

A certain Mr. Valentine Kittering, of Dauphin County, has communicated to the Senate of Pennsylvania a sure remedy for the bite of any kind of mad animals. He says that his ancestors had already used it in Germany 250 years ago, and that he had always found it to answer the purpose, during a residence of fifty years in the United States. He only published it from motives of humanity. This remedy consists in a weed called *Chick-weed*. It is a summer plant, known to the Germans and Swiss by the names of *Gauch-neil, Rothea Meyer,* or *Rother Huehnerdarm.* In England it is called *Red Pimpernel;* and its botanical name is *Angelica Phonicea.* It must be gathered in June when in full bloom and dried in the shade, and then pulverized. The dose of this for a grown person is a small tablespoonful, or in weight a drachm and a scruple, at once, in beer or water. For children the dose is the same, yet it must be administered at three different times. In applying it to animals, it must be used green, cut to pieces and mixed with bran or other feed. For the hogs the pulverized weed is made into little balls by mixing it with flour and water. It can also be put on bread and butter, or in honey, molasses, etc. The Rev. Henry Muhlenberg says that in Germany 30 grains of this powder are given four times a day, the first day, then one dose a day for a whole week; while at the same time the wound is washed out with a decoction of the weed, and then the powder strewed in it. Mr. Kittering says that he in all instances administered but one dose, with the most happy results. This is said to be the same remedy through which the late Doctor William Stoy effected so many cures.

A VERY GOOD MEANS TO INCREASE THE GROWTH OF WOOL ON SHEEP, AND TO PREVENT DISEASE AMONG THEM.

William Ellis, in his excellent work on the English manner of raising sheep, relates the following: I know a tenant who had a flock of sheep that produced an unusual quantity of wool. He informed me that he was in the habit of washing his sheep with buttermilk just after shearing them, which was the cause of the unusual growth of wool; because it is a known fact that buttermilk does not only improve the growth of sheep's wool, but also of the hair of other animals. Those who have no buttermilk may substitute common milk, mixed with salt and water, which will answer nearly as well to wash the sheep just sheared. And I guarantee that by rightly applying this means, you will not only have a great increase of wool, but the sheep-lice and their entire brood will be destroyed. It also cures all manner of scab and itch, and prevents them from taking cold.

A WELL-TRIED PLASTER TO REMOVE MORTIFICATION.

Take six hen's eggs and boil them in hot ashes until they are right hard; then take the yellow of the eggs and fry them in a gill of lard until they are quite black; then put a handful of rue with it, and afterward filter it through a cloth. When this is done add a gill of sweet oil to it.

It will take most effect where the plaster for a female is prepared by a male, and the plaster for a male prepared by a female.

A GOOD REMEDY FOR THE POLL-EVIL IN HORSES.

Take white turpentine, rub it over the poll-evil with your hand, and then melt it with a hot iron, so that it runs into the wound. After this take neatsfoot oil or goose grease and rub it into the wound in the same manner, and for three days in succession, commencing on the last Friday of the last quarter of the moon.

FOR THE SCURVY AND SORE THROAT.

Speak the following, and it will certainly help you: Job went through the land, holding his staff close in the hand, when God the Lord did meet him, and said to him: Job, what are thou grieved at? Job said: Oh God, why should I not be sad? My throat and my mouth are rotting away. Then said the Lord to Job: In yonder valley there is a well which will cure thee [name], and thy mouth, and thy throat, in the name of God the Father, the Son and the Holy Ghost. Amen.

This must be spoken three times in the morning and three times in the evening; and where it reads "which will cure," you must blow three times in the child's mouth.

A VERY GOOD PLASTER.

Take wormwood, rue, medels, sheeprip-wort, pointy plantain, in equal proportions, a larger proportion of bees'-wax and tallow, and some spirits of turpentine; put it together in a pot, boil it well, and then strain it, and you have a very good plaster.

TO STOP BLEEDING.

I walk through a green forest;
There I find three wells, cool and cold;
The first is called courage,
The second is called good,
And the third is called stop the blood.

† † †

ANOTHER WAY TO STOP BLEEDING, AND TO HEAL WOUNDS IN MAN AS WELL AS ANIMALS.

On Christ's grave there grows three roses; the first is kind, the second is valued among the rulers, and the third says: blood, thou must stop, and wound, thou must heal. Everything prescribed for man in this book is also applicable to animals.

FOR GAINING A LAWFUL SUIT.

It reads, if anyone has to settle any just claim by way of a law suit let him take some of the largest kind of sage and write the name of the twelve apostles on the leaves, and put them in his shoes before entering the courthouse, and he shall certainly gain the suit.

FOR THE SWELLING OF CATTLE.

To Desh break no Flesh, but to Desh! While saying this, run your hand along the back of the animal.   † † †

NOTE.—The hand must be put upon the bare skin in all cases of using sympathetic words.

AN EASY METHOD OF CATCHING FISH.

In a vessel of white glass must be put: 8 grains of civit, (musk), and as much castorium; two ounces of eel-fat, and 4 ounces of unsalted butter; after which the vessel must be well closed, and put in some place where it will keep moderately warm for nine or ten days, and then the composition must be well stirred with a stick until it is perfectly mixed.

APPLICATION.—1. *In using the hooks.*—Worms or insects used for baiting the hooks must first be moistened with this composition, and then put in a bladder or box, which may be carried in the pocket.

2. *In using the net.*—Small balls formed of the soft part of fresh bread must be dipped in this composition and then by means of thread fastened inside of the net before throwing it into the water.

3. *Catching Fish with the Hands.*—Besmear your legs or boots with this composition before entering the water at the place where the fish are expected, and they will collect in great numbers around you.

A VERY GOOD AND SAFE REMEDY FOR RHEUMATISM.

From one to two dollars have often been paid for this recipe alone, it being the best and surest remedy to cure the rheumatism. Let it be known therefore: Take a piece of cloth, some tape and thread, neither of which must ever have been in water; the thread must not have a single knot in it, and the cloth and tape must have been spun by a child not quite or at least not more than seven years of age. The letter given below must be carefully sewed in the piece of cloth, and tied around the neck, unbeshrewdly, on the first Friday in the decreasing moon; and immediately after hanging it around the neck, the Lord's prayer and the articles of faith must be repeated. What now follows must be written in the before-mentioned letter:

"May God the Father, Son and Holy Ghost grant it, Amen. Seek immediately, and seek; thus commandeth the Lord thy God, through the first man whom God did love upon earth. Seek immediately, and seek; thus commandeth the Lord thy God, through Luke, the Evangelist, and through Paul, the Apostle. Seek immediately, and seek; thus commandeth the Lord thy God, through the twelve messengers. Seek immediately, and seek; thus commandeth the Lord thy God by the first man that God might be loved. Seek immediately, and convulse; thus commandeth the Lord thy God, through the Holy Fathers, who have been made by divine and holy writ. Seek immediately, and convulse; thus commandeth the Lord thy God, through the dear and holy angels, and through his paternal and divine Omnipotence, and his heavenly confidence and endurance. Seek immediately, and convulse; thus commandeth the Lord thy God, through the burning oven which was preserved by the blessing of God. Seek immediately, and convulse; thus commandeth the Lord thy God, through all power and might, through the prophet Jonah who was preserved in the belly of the whale for three days and three nights, by the blessing of God. Seek immediately and convulse; thus commandeth the Lord thy God, through all the power and might which proceed from divine humility, and in all-eternity; whereby no harm be done unto † N † nor unto any part of his body be they the ravenous convulsions, or the yellow convulsions, or the white convulsions, or the red convulsions, or the black convulsions, or by whatever name convulsions may be called; these all shall do no harm unto thee † N † nor unto any part of thy body, nor to thy head, nor to thy neck, nor to thy heart, nor to thy stomach, nor to any of thy veins, nor to thy arms, nor to thy legs, nor to thy eyes, nor to thy tongue, nor to any part or parcel of thy body. This I write for thee † N † in these words, and in the name of God the Father, Son and Holy Ghost. Amen. God bless it. Amen."

Notice.—If anyone write such a letter for another, the Christian name of the person must be mentioned in it; as you will observe, where the N stands singly in the above letter, there must be the name.

A GOOD WAY TO DESTROY WORMS IN BEE-HIVES.

With very little trouble and at an expense of a quarter-dollar, you can certainly free your bee-hives from worms for a whole year. Get from an apothecary store the powder called *Pensses Blum*, which will not injure the bees in the

least. The application of it is as follows: For one bee-hive
you take as much of this powder as the point of your knife
will hold, mix it with one ounce of good whiskey, and put
it in a common vial; then make a hole in the bee-hive and
pour it in thus mixed with the whiskey, which is sufficient
for one hive at once. Make the hole so that it can be easily
poured in. As said before, a quarter dollar's worth of this
powder is enough for one hive.

RECIPE FOR MAKING A PASTE TO PREVENT GUN-BARRELS FROM RUSTING, WHETHER IRON OR STEEL.

Take an ounce of bear's fat, half an ounce of badger's
grease, half an ounce of snake's fat, one ounce of almond
oil, and a quarter of an ounce of pulverized indigo, and melt
it altogether in a new vessel over a fire, stir it well, and
put it afterward into some vessel. In using it, a lump as
large as a common nut must be put upon a piece of woollen
cloth and then rubbed on the barrel and lock of the gun,
and it will keep the barrel from rusting.

TO MAKE A WICK WHICH IS NEVER CONSUMED.

Take an ounce of asbestos and boil it in a quart of strong
lye for two hours; then pour off the lye and clarify what
remains by pouring rain-water on it three or four times,
after which you can form a wick from it which will never
be consumed by the fire.

A MORNING PRAYER TO BE SPOKEN BEFORE STARTING ON A JOURNEY, WHICH WILL SAVE THE PERSON FROM ALL MISHAPS.

I (here the name is to be pronounced) will go on a journey today; I will walk upon God's way, and walk where
God himself did walk, and our dear Lord Jesus Christ, and
our dearest Virgin with her dear little babe, with her seven
rings and her true things. Oh, thou! my dear Lord Jesus
Christ, I am thine own, that no dog may bite me, no wolf
bite me, and no murder secretly approach me; save me, O
my God, from sudden death! I am in God's hands, and
there I will bind myself. In God's hands I am by our Lord
Jesus' five wounds, that any gun or other arms may not
do me any more harm than the virginity of our Holy Virgin
Mary was injured by the favor of her beloved Jesus. After
this say three Lord's prayers, the Ave Maria, and the articles
of faith.

A SAFE AND APPROVED MEANS TO BE APPLIED IN CASES OF FIRE AND PESTILENCE.

Welcome, thou fiery fiend! do not extend further than thou already hast. This I count unto thee as a repentant act, in the name of God the Father, the Son and the Holy Ghost.

I command unto thee, fire, by the power of God, which createth and worketh everything, that thou now do cease, and not extend any further as certainly as Christ was standing on the Jordan's stormy banks, being baptized by John the holy man.

This I count unto thee as a repentant act in the name of the holy Trinity.

I command unto thee, fire, by the power of God, now to abate thy flames; as certainly as Mary retained her virginity before all ladies who retained theirs, so chaste and pure; therefore, fire, cease thy wrath.

This I count unto thee as a repentant act in the name of the holy Trinity.

I command unto thee fire, to abate thy heat, by the precious blood of Jesus Christ, which he has shed for us, and our sins and transgressions.

This I count unto thee, fire, as a repentant act, in the name of God the Father, the Son and the Holy Ghost.

Jesus of Nazareth, a king of the Jews, help us from this dangerous fire, and guard this land and its bounds from all epidemic disease and pestilence.

REMARKS.—This has been discovered by a Christian Gypsy King of Egypt. Anno 1740, on the 10th of June, six gypsies were executed on the gallows in the kingdom of Prussia. The seventh of their party was a man of eighty years of age and was to be executed by the sword on the 16th of the same month. But fortunately for him, quite unexpectedly, a conflagration broke out, and the old Gypsy was taken to the fire to try his arts, which he successfully did to the great surprise of all present, by bespeaking the conflagration in a manner that it wholly or entirely ceased and disappeared in less than ten minutes. Upon this, the proof having been given in day-time, he received pardon and was set at liberty. This was confirmed and attested by the government of the King of Prussia, and the General Superintendent at Kœnigsberg, and given to the public in print. It was first published at Kœnigsberg in Prussia, by Alexander Bausman, Anno 1745.

Whoever has this letter in his house will be free from all danger of fire, as well as from lightning. If a pregnant woman carries this letter about her, neither enchantment nor evil spirits can injure her or her child. Further, if anybody has this letter in his house, or carries it about his person, he will be safe from the injuries of pestilence.

While saying these sentences, one must pass three times around the fire. This has availed in all instances.

TO PREVENT CONFLAGRATION.

Take a black chicken, in the morning or evening, cut its head off and throw it upon the ground; cut its stomach out, yet leave it altogether; then try to get a piece of a shirt which was worn by a chaste virgin during her terms, and cut out a piece as large as a common dish from that part which is bloodiest. These two things wrap up together, then try to get an egg which was laid on maunday Thursday. These three things put together in wax; then put them in a pot holding eight quarts, and bury it under the threshold of your house, with the aid of God, and as long as there remains a single stick of your house together, no conflagration will happen. If your house should happen to be on fire already in front and behind, the fire will nevertheless do no injury to you nor to your children. This is done by the power of God, and is quite certain and infallible. If fire should break out unexpectedly, then try to get a whole shirt in which your servant-maid had her terms or a sheet on which a child was born, and throw it into the fire, wrapped up in a bundle, and without saying anything. This will certainly stop it.

TO PREVENT WITCHES FROM BEWITCHING CATTLE, TO BE WRITTEN AND PLACED IN THE STABLE; AND AGAINST BAD MEN AND EVIL SPIRITS WHICH NIGHTLY TORMENT OLD AND YOUNG PEOPLE, TO BE WRITTEN AND PLACED ON THE BEDSTEAD.

"Trotter Head, I forbid thee my house and premises; I forbid thee my horse and cow-stable; I forbid thee my bedstead, that thou mayest not breathe upon me; breathe into some other house, until thou hast ascended every hill, until thou hast counted every fence-post, and until thou hast crossed every water. And thus dear day may come again into my house, in the name of God the Father, the Son, and the Holy Ghost. Amen."

This will certainly protect and free all persons and animals from witchcraft.

TO EXTINGUISH FIRE WITHOUT WATER.

Write the following words on each side of a plate, and throw it into the fire, and it will be extinguished forthwith:

```
S A T O R
A R E P O
T E N E T
O P E R A
R O T A S
```

TO PREVENT BAD PEOPLE FROM GETTING ABOUT THE CATTLE

Take wormwood, gith, five-finger weed, and assafœtida; three cents' worth of each; the straw of horse beans, some dirt swept together behind the door of the stable and a little salt. Tie these all up together with a tape, and put the bundle in a hole about the threshold over which your cattle pass in and out, and cover it well with lignum-vitæ wood. This will certainly be of use.

ANOTHER METHOD OF STOPPING FIRE.

Our dear Sarah journeyed through the land, having a fiery hot brand in her hand. The fiery brand heats; the fiery brand sweats. Fiery brand, stop your heat; fiery brand, stop your sweat.

HOW TO FASTEN OR SPELL-BIND ANYTHING.

You say, "Christ's cross and Christ's crown, Christ Jesus' colored blood, be thou every hour good. God, the Father, is before me; God, the Son, is beside me; God, the Holy Ghost, is behind me. Whoever now is stronger than these three persons may come, by day or night, to attack me."

† † †

Then say the Lord's prayer three times.

ANOTHER WAY OF FASTENING OR SPELL-BINDING.

After repeating the above, you speak, "At every step may Jesus walk with [name]. He is my head; I am his limb; therefore, Jesus, be with [name].

A BENEDICTION TO PREVENT FIRE.

"The bitter sorrows and the death of our dear Lord Jesus Christ shall prevail. Fire and wind and great heat and all that is within the power of these elements, I command thee, through the Lord Jesus Christ, who has spoken to the winds and the waters, and they obeyed him. By these powerful words spoken by Jesus, I command, threaten, and inform

thee, fire, flame, and heat, and your powers as elements, to
flee forthwith. The holy, rosy blood of our dear Lord Jesus
Christ may rule it. Thou, fire, and wind, and great heat, I
command thee, as the Lord did, by his holy angels, command
the great heat in the firey oven to leave those three holy
men, Shadrack and his companions, Meshach and Abednego,
untouched, which was done accordingly. Thus thou shalt
abate, thou fire, flame, and great heat, the Almighty God
having spoken in creating the four elements, together with
heaven and earth; Fiat! Fiat! Fiat! that is: It shall be in
the name of God the Father, the Son, and the Holy Ghost.
Amen.

HOW TO RELIEVE PERSONS OR ANIMALS AFTER BEING BEWITCHED.

Three false tongues have bound thee, three holy tongues
have spoken for thee. The first is God the Father, the second
is God the Son, and the third is God the Holy Ghost. They
will give you blood and flesh, peace and comfort. Flesh and
blood are grown upon thee, born on thee, and lost on thee.
If any man trample on thee with his horse, God will bless
thee, and the holy Ciprian; has any woman trampled on
thee, God and the body of Mary shall bless thee; if any
servant has given you trouble, I bless thee through God and
the laws of heaven; if any servant-maid or woman has led
you astray, God and the heavenly constellations shall bless
thee. Heaven is above thee, the earth is beneath thee, and
thou art between. I bless thee against all tramplings by
horses. Our dear Lord Jesus Christ walked about in his bitter afflictions and death; and all the Jews that had spoken and
promised, trembled in their falsehoods and mockery. Look,
now trembleth the Son of God, as if he had the itch, said
the Jews. And then spake Jesus: I have not the itch and
no one shall have it. Whoever will assist me to carry the
cross, him will I free from the itch, in the name of God
the Father, the Son, and the Holy Ghost. Amen.

TO PROTECT HOUSES AND PREMISES AGAINST SICKNESS AND THEFT.

Ito, alto Massa Dandi Bando, III. Amen.

J. R. N. R. J.

Our Lord Jesus Christ stepped into the hall, and the Jews
searched him everywhere. Thus shalt those who now speak
evil of me with their false tongues, and contend against me,
one day bear sorrows, be silenced, dumbstruck, intimi-

dated, and abused, forever and ever, by the glory of God. The glory of God shall assist me in this. Do thou aid me J. J. J. forever and ever. Amen.

AGAINST DANGERS AND MISHAPS IN THE HOUSE.

Sanct Matheus, Sanct Marcus, Sanct Lucas, Sanct Johannis.

A DIRECTION FOR A GYPSY SENTENCE, TO BE CARRIED ABOUT THE PERSON AS A PROTECTION UNDER ALL CIRCUMSTANCES.

Like unto the prophet Jonas, as a type of Christ, who was guarded for three days and three nights in the belly of a whale, thus shall the Almighty God, as a Father, guard and protect me from all evil. J. J. J.

AGAINST EVIL SPIRITS AND ALL MANNER OF WITCHCRAFT.

I.

N. I. R.

I.

SANCTUS SPIRITUS.

I.

N. I. R.

I.

All this be guarded here in time, and there in eternity. Amen.

You must write all the above on a piece of white paper and carry it about you. The characters or letters above signify: "God bless me here in time, and there eternally."

AGAINST SWELLINGS.

"Three pure virgins went out on a journey to inspect a swelling and sickness. The first one said, It is hoarse. The second said, It is not. The third said, If it is not, then will our Lord Jesus Christ come." This must be spoken in the name of the Holy Trinity.

HOW TO TREAT A COW AFTER THE MILK IS TAKEN FROM HER.

Give to the cow three spoonfuls of her last milk, and say to the spirits in her blood: "Ninny has done it, and I have swallowed her in the name of God the Father, the Son, and the Holy Ghost. Amen." Pray what you choose at the same time.

AGAINST ADVERSITIES AND ALL MANNER OF CONTENTION.

Power, hero, Prince of Peace, J. J. J.

AGAINST DANGER AND DEATH, TO BE CARRIED ABOUT THE PERSON.

I know that my Redeemer liveth, and that he will call me from the grave, etc.

ANOTHER METHOD OF TREATING A SICK COW.

J. The cross of Jesus Christ poured out milk;

J. The cross of Jesus Christ poured out water;

J. The cross of Jesus Christ has poured them out.

These lines must be written on three pieces of white paper; then take the milk of the sick cow and these three pieces of paper, put them in a pot, and scrape a little of the skull of a criminal; close it well, and put it over a hot fire, and the witch will have to die. If you take the three pieces of paper, with the writing on them, in your mouth and go out before your house, speak three times, and then give them to your cattle, you shall not only see all the witches, but your cattle will also get well again.

AGAINST THE FEVER.

Pray early in the morning, and then turn your shirt around the left sleeve, and say: Turn, thou, shirt, and thou, fever, do likewise turn. (Do not forget to mention the name of the person having the fever). This, I tell thee, for thy repentance sake, in the name of God the Father, the Son, and the Holy Ghost. Amen. If you repeat this for three successive mornings the fever will disappear.

TO SPELL-BIND A THIEF SO THAT HE CANNOT STIR.

This benediction must be spoken on a Thursday morning, before sunrise and in the open air:

"Thus shall rule it, God the Father, the Son, and the Holy Ghost. Amen. Thirty-three Angels speak to each other coming to administer in company with Mary. Then spoke dear Daniel, the holy one: Trust, my dear woman, I see some thieves coming who intend stealing your dear babe; this I cannot conceal from you. Then spake our dear Lady to Saint Peter: I have bound with a band, through Christ's hand; therefore, my thieves are bound even by the hand of Christ, if they wish to steal mine own, in the house, in the chest, upon the meadow or fields, in the woods, in the orchard, in the vineyard, or in the garden, or wherever they intend to steal. Our dear Lady said: Whoever chooses may steal; yet if anyone does steal, he shall stand like a buck, he shall stand like a stake, and shall count all the stones upon the earth, and all the stars in the heavens. Thus I give thee leave, and command every spirit to be master over every thief, by the guardianship of Saint Daniel, and by the burden of this world's goods. And the countenance shall be unto thee, that thou canst not move from the spot, as long as my tongue in the flesh shall not give thee leave. This I command thee by the Holy Virgin Mary, the Mother of God, by the power and might by which he has created heaven and earth, by the host of all the angels, and by all the saints of God the Father, the Son, and the Holy Ghost. Amen." If you wish to set the thief free, you must tell him to leave in the name of St. John.

ANOTHER WAY TO SPELL-BIND THIEVES.

Ye thieves, I conjure you, to be obedient like Jesus Christ, who obeyed his Heavenly Father unto the cross, and to stand without moving out of my sight, in the name of the Trinity. I command you by the power of God and the incarnation of Jesus Christ, not to move out of my sight, † † † like Jesus Christ was standing on Jordan's stormy banks to be baptized by John. And furthermore, I conjure you, horse and rider, to stand still and not to move out of my sight, like Jesus Christ did stand when he was about to be nailed to the cross to release the fathers of the church from the bonds of hell. Ye thieves, I bind you with the same bonds with which Jesus our Lord has bound hell; and thus ye shall be bound; † † † and the same words that bind you shall also release you.

TO EFFECT THE SAME IN LESS TIME.

Thou horseman and footman, you are coming under your hats; you are scattered! With the blood of Jesus Christ, with his five holy wounds, thy barrel, thy gun, and thy pistol are bound; sabre, sword, and knife are enchanted and bound, in the name of God the Father, the Son, and the Holy Ghost. Amen.

This must be spoken three times.

TO RELEASE SPELL-BOUND PERSONS.

You horseman and footman, whom I here conjure at this time, you may pass on in the name of Jesus Christ, through the word of God and the will of Christ; ride ye now and pass.

TO COMPEL A THIEF TO RETURN STOLEN GOODS.

Early in the morning before sunrise you must go to a pear tree, and take with you three nails out of a coffin, or three horse-shoe nails that were never used, and holding these toward the rising sun, you must say:

"Oh, thief, I bind you by the first nail, which I drive into thy skull and thy brain, to return the goods thou hast stolen to their former place; thou shalt feel as sick and as anxious to see men, and to see the place you stole from, as felt the disciple Judas after betraying Jesus. I bind thee by the other nail, which I drive into your lungs and liver, to return the stolen goods to their former place; thou shall feel as sick and as anxious to see men, and to see the place you have stolen from, as did Pilate in the fires of hell. The third nail I shall drive into thy foot, oh thief, in order that thou shalt return the stolen goods to the very same place from which thou hast stolen them. Oh, thief, I bind thee and compel thee, by the three holy nails which were driven through the hands and feet of Jesus Christ, to return the stolen goods to the very same place from which thou hast stolen them. † † † The three nails, however, must be greased with the grease from an executed criminal or other sinful person.

A BENEDICTION FOR ALL PURPOSES.

Jesus, I will arise; Jesus, do thou accompany me; Jesus, do thou lock my heart into thine, and let my body and my soul be commended unto thee. The Lord is crucified. May God guard my senses that evil spirits may not overcome me, in the name of God the Father, Son, and the Holy Ghost. Amen.

TO WIN EVERY GAME ONE ENGAGES IN.

Tie the heart of a bat with a red silken string to the right arm, and you will win every game at cards you play.

AGAINST BURNS.

Our dear Lord Jesus Christ going on a journey, saw a firebrand burning; it was Saint Lorenzo stretched out on a roast. He rendered him assistance and consolation; he lifted his divine hand and blessed the brand; he stopped it from spreading deeper and wider. Thus may the burning be blessed in the name of God the Father, Son and Holy Ghost. Amen.

ANOTHER REMEDY FOR BURNS.

Clear out, brand, but never in; be thou cold or hot, thou must cease to burn. May God guard thy blood and thy flesh, thy marrow and thy bones, and every artery, great or small. They all shall be guarded and protected in the name of God against inflammation and mortification, in the name of God the Father, the Son, and the Holy Ghost. Amen.

A BENEDICTION AGAINST WORMS.

Peter and Jesus went out upon the fields; they ploughed three furrows, and ploughed up three worms. The one was white, the other was black, and the third one was red. Now all the worms are dead, in the name † † † Repeat these words three times.

TO BE GIVEN TO CATTLE AGAINST WITCHCRAFT.

```
S A T O R
A R E P O
T E N E T
O P E R A
R O T A S
```

This must be written on paper and the cattle made to swallow it in their feed.

HOW TO TIE UP AND HEAL WOUNDS.

Speak the following: "This wound I tie up in three names, in order that thou mayest take from it heat, water, falling off of the flesh, swelling, and all that may be injurious about the swelling, in the name of the Holy Trinity." This must be spoken three times; then draw a string three times around the wound, and put it under the corner of the house toward the East, and say: "I put thee there, † † † in order that thou mayest take unto thyself the gathered water, the swelling, and the running, and all that may be injurious about the wound. Amen." Then repeat the Lord's Prayer and some good hymn.

TO TAKE THE PAIN OUT OF A FRESH WOUND.

Our dear Lord Jesus Christ had a great many biles and wounds, and yet he never had them dressed. They did not grow old, they were not cut, nor were they ever found running. Jonas was blind, and I spoke to the heavenly child, as true as five holy wounds were inflicted.

AGAINST EVERY EVIL INFLUENCE.

Lord Jesus, thy wounds so red will guard me against death.

TO RETAIN THE RIGHT IN COURT AND COUNCIL.

Jesus Nazarenus, Rex Judeorum.

First carry these characters with you, written on paper, and then repeat the following words: "I [*name*] appear before the house of the Judge. Three dead men look out of the window; one having no tongue, the other having no lungs, and the third was sick, blind and dumb." This is intended to be used when you are standing before a court in your right, and the judge not being favorably disposed toward you. While on your way to court you must repeat the benediction already given above.

TO STOP BLEEDING AT ANY TIME.

Write the name of the four principal waters of the whole world, flowing out of Paradise, on a paper, namely: Pison, Gihon, Hedekiel and Pheat, and put it on the wound. In the first book of Moses, the second chapter, verses 11, 12, 13, you will find them. You will find this effective.

ANOTHER WAY TO STOP BLOOD.

As soon as you cut yourself you must say: "Blessed wound, blessed hour, blessed be the day on which Jesus Christ was born, in the name † † † Amen.

ANOTHER SIMILAR PRESCRIPTION.

Breathe three times upon the patient, and say the Lord's Prayer three times until the words, "upon the earth," and the bleeding will be stopped.

ANOTHER STILL MORE CERTAIN WAY TO STOP BLEEDING.

If the bleeding will not stop, or if a vein has been cut, then lay the following on it, and it will stop that hour. Yet if anyone does not believe this, let him write the letters upon a knife and stab an irrational animal, and he will not be able to draw blood. And whosoever carries this about him will be safe against all his enemies.

I. m. I. K. I. B. I. P. a. x. v. ss. Ss. vas,

I. P. O. unay Lit. Dom. mper vobism.

And whenever a woman is going to give birth to a child, or is otherwise afflicted, let her have this letter about her person; it will certainly be of avail.

A PECULIAR SIGN TO KEEP BACK MEN AND ANIMALS.

Whenever you are in danger of being attacked, then carry this sign with you: "In the name of God, I make the attack. May it please my Redeemer to assist me. Upon the holy assistance of God I depend entirely; upon the holy assistance of God and my gun I rely very truly. God alone be with us. Blessed be Jesus.

PROTECTION OF ONE'S HOUSE AND HEARTH.

Beneath thy guardianship I am safe against all tempests and all enemies, J. J. J.

These three J's signify *Jesus* three times.

A CHARM TO BE CARRIED ABOUT THE PERSON.

Carry these words about you, and nothing can hit you: Ananiah, Azariah, and Misæl, blessed be the Lord, for he has redeemed us from hell, and has saved us from death, and he has redeemed us out of the fiery furnace, and has preserved us even in the midst of the fire; in the same manner may it please him the Lord that there be no fire.

I.

N. I. R.

I.

TO CHARM ENEMIES, ROBBERS AND MURDERERS.

God be with you, brethren; stop, ye thieves, robbers, murderers, horsemen, and soldiers, in all humility, for we have tasted the rosy blood of Jesus. Your rifles and guns will be stopped up with the holy blood of Jesus; and all swords and arms are made harmless by the five holy wounds of Jesus. There are three roses upon the heart of God; the first is beneficent, the other is omnipotent, the third is his holy will. You thieves must therefore stand under it, standing still as long as I will. In the name of God the Father, Son and Holy Ghost, you are conjured and made to stand.

A CHARM AGAINST FIRE-ARMS.

Jesus passed over the Red Sea, and looked upon the land; and thus must break all ropes and bands, and thus must break all manner of fire-arms, rifles, guns, or pistols, and all false tongues be silenced. May the benediction of God on creating the first man always be upon me; the benediction spoken by God, when he ordered in a dream that Joseph and Mary together with Jesus should flee into Egypt, be upon me always, and may the holy † be ever lovely and beloved in my right hand. I journey through the country at large where no one is robbed, killed or murdered—where no one can do me an injury, and where not even a dog could bite me, or any other animal tear me to pieces. In all things let me be protected, as also my flesh and blood, against sins and false tongues which reach from the earth up to heaven, by the power of the four Evangelists, in the name of God the Father, God the Son, and God the Holy Ghost. Amen.

ANOTHER FOR THE SAME.

I [*name*] conjure ye guns, swords and knives, as well as all other kinds of arms, by the spear that pierced the side of God, and opened it so that blood and water could flow out, that ye do not injure me, a servant of God, in the † † †. I conjure ye, by Saint Stephen, who was stoned by the Virgin, that ye cannot injure me who am a servant of God, in the name of † † †. Amen.

PROTECTION AGAINST ALL KINDS OF WEAPONS.

Jesus, God and man, do thou protect me against all manner of guns, fire-arms, long or short, of any kind of metal. Keep thou thy fire, like the Virgin Mary, who kept her fire both before and after her birth. May Christ bind up all fire-arms after the manner of his having bound up himself in humility while in the flesh. Jesus, do thou render harmless all arms and weapons, like unto the husband of Mary the mother of God, he having been harmless likewise. Furthermore, do thou guard the three holy drops of blood which Christ sweated on the Mount of Olives. Jesus Christ! do thou protect me against being killed and against burning fires. Jesus, do thou not suffer me to be killed, much less to be damned, without having received the Lord's Supper. May God the Father, Son, and Holy Ghost, assist me in this. Amen.

A CHARM AGAINST SHOOTING, CUTTING OR THRUSTING.

In the name of J. J. J. Amen. I [*name*]; Jesus Christ is the true salvation; Jesus Christ governs, reigns, defeats and conquers every enemy, visible or invisible; Jesus, be thou with me at all times, forever and ever, upon all roads and ways, upon the water and the land, on the mountain and in the valley, in the house and in the yard, in the whole world wherever I am, stand, run, ride or drive; whether I sleep or wake, eat or drink, there be thou also, Lord Jesus Christ, at all times, late and early, every hour, every moment; and in all my goings in or goings out. Those five holy red wounds, oh, Lord Jesus Christ, may they guard me against all fire-arms, be they secret or public, that they cannot injure me or do me any harm whatever, in the name of † † †. May Jesus Christ, with his guardianship and protection, shield me [*name*] always from daily commission of sins, worldly injuries and injustice, from contempt, from pestilence and other diseases, from fear, torture, and great suffering, from all evil intentions, from false tongues and old clatter-brains; and that no kind of fire-arms can inflict any injury to my body, do thou take care of me. † † †. And that no band of thieves nor Gypsies, highway robbers, incendiaries, witches and other evil spirits may secretly enter my house or premises, nor break in; may the dear Virgin Mary, and all children who are in heaven with God, in eternal joys, protect and guard me against them; and the glory of God the Father shall strengthen me, the wisdom of God the Son shall enlighten me, and the grace of God the Holy

Ghost shall empower me from this hour unto all eternity. Amen.

TO CHARM GUNS AND OTHER ARMS.

The blessing which came from heaven at the birth of Christ be with me [*name*]. The blessing of God at the creation of the first man be with me; the blessing of Christ on being imprisoned, bound, lashed, crowned so dreadfully, and beaten, and dying on the cross, be with me; the blessing which the Priest spoke over the tender, joyful corpse of our Lord Jesus Christ, be with me; the constancy of the Holy Mary and all the saints of God, of the three holy kings, Casper, Melchoir and Balthasar, be with me; the holy four Evangelists, Matthew, Mark, Luke and John, be with me; the Archangels St. Michæl, St. Gabriel, St. Raphæl and St. Uriel, be with me; the twelve holy messengers of the Patriarchs and all the Hosts of Heaven, be with me; and the inexpressible number of all the Saints be with me. Amen.

Papa, R. tarn, Tetregammate Angen.

Jesus Nazarenus, Rex Judeorum.

TO PREVENT BEING CHEATED, CHARMED OR BEWITCHED, AND TO BE AT ALL TIMES BLESSED.

Like unto the cup and the wine, and the holy supper, which our dear Lord Jesus Christ gave unto his dear disciples on Maunday Thursday, may the Lord Jesus guard me in day-time, and at night, that no dog may bite me, no wild beast tear me to pieces, no tree fall on me, no water rise against me, no fire-arms injure me, no weapons, no steel, no iron, cut me, no fire burn me, no false sentence fall upon me, no false tongue injure me, no rogue enrage me, and that no fiends, no witchcraft and enchantment can harm me. Amen.

DIFFERENT DIRECTIONS TO EFFECT THE SAME.

The Holy Trinity guard me, and be and remain with me on the water and upon the land, in the water or in the fields, in cities or villages, in the whole world wherever I am. The Lord Jesus Christ protect me against all my enemies, secret or public; and may the Eternal Godhead also guard me through the bitter sufferings of Jesus Christ; his holy rosy blood, shed on the cross, assist me, J. J. Jesus has been crucified, tortured and died. These are true words, and in the same way must all words be efficacious which are here put down, and spoken in prayer by me. This shall assist me that I shall not be imprisoned, bound or overcome by anyone. Before me all guns or other weapons shall be of no use or power. Fire-arms, hold your fire in the almighty hand of God. Thus all fire-arms shall be charmed. † † †. When the right hand of the Lord Jesus Christ was fastened to the tree of the cross; like unto the Son of the Heavenly Father who was obedient unto death, may the Eternal God-head protect me by the rosy blood, by the five holy wounds on the tree of the cross; and thus must I be blessed and well protected like the cup and the wine, and the genuine true bread, which Jesus Christ gave to his disciples on the evening of Maunday Thursday. J. J. J.

ANOTHER SIMILAR DIRECTION.

The grace of God and his benevolence be with me (N). I shall now ride or walk out; and I will gird about my loins with a sure ring. So it pleases God, the Heavenly Father, he will protect me, my flesh and blood, and all my arteries and limbs, during this day and night which I have before me; and however numerous my enemies might be, they must be dumbstruck, and all become like a dead man, white as snow, so that no one will be able to shoot, cut or throw at me, or to overcome me, although he may hold rifle or steel against whosoever else evil weapons and arms might be called, in his hand. My rifle shall go off like the lightning from heaven, and my sword shall cut like a razor. Then went our dear lady Mary upon a very high mountain; she looked down into a very dusky valley and beheld her dear child standing amidst the Jews, harsh, very harsh, because he was bound so harsh, because he was bound so hard; and therefore may the dear Lord Jesus Christ save me from all that is injurious to me. † † † Amen.

ANOTHER SIMILAR DIRECTION.

There walk out during this day and night, that thou mayest not let any of my enemies, or thieves, approach me, if they do not intend to bring me what was spent from the holy altar. Because God the Lord Jesus Christ is ascended into heaven in his living body. O Lord, this is good for me this day and night. † † † Amen.

ANOTHER ONE LIKE IT.

In the name of God I walk out. God the Father be with me, and God the Holy Ghost be by my side. Whoever is stronger than these three persons may approach my body and my life; yet whoso is not stronger than these three would much better let me be. J. J. J.

ANOTHER ONE LIKE IT.

I conjure thee, sword, sabre or knife, that mightest injure or harm me, by the priest of all prayers, who had gone into the temple at Jerusalem, and said: An edged sword shall pierce your soul that you may not injure me, who am a child of God.

A VERY EFFECTIVE CHARM.

I [*name*] conjure thee, sword or knife, as well as all other weapons, by that spear which pierced Jesus' side, and opened it to the gushing out of blood and water, that he keep me from injury as one of the servants of God. † † † Amen.

A VERY SAFE AND RELIABLE CHARM.

The peace of our Lord Jesus Christ be with me [*name*]. Oh shot, stand still! in the name of the mighty prophets Agtion and Alias, and do not kill me! oh shot, stop short. I conjure you by heaven and earth, and by the last judgment, that you do no harm unto me, a child of God. † † †

A GOOD CHARM AGAINST THIEVES.

There are three lilies standing upon the grave of the Lord our God; the first one is the courage of God, the other is the blood of God, and the third one is the will of God. Stand still, thief! No more than Jesus Christ stepped down from the cross, no more shalt thou move from this spot; this I command thee by the four evangelists and elements of heaven, there in the river, or in the shot, or in the judgment, or in the sight. Thus I conjure you by the last judgment to stand still and not to move, until I see all the stars in heaven and the sun rises again. Thus I stop by running and jumping and command it in the name of † † †. Amen.

This must be repeated three times.

HOW TO RECOVER STOLEN GOODS.

Take good care to notice through which door the thief passed out, and cut off three small chips from the posts of that door; then take these three chips to a wagon, unbeshrewdly, however; take off one of the wheels and put the three chips into the stock of the wheel, in the three highest names, then turn the wheel backwards and say: Thief, thief, thief! Turn back with the stolen goods; thou art forced to do it by the Almighty power of God: † † †. God the Father calls thee back, God the Son turns thee back so that thou must return, and God the Holy Ghost leads thee back, until thou arrive at the place from which thou hast stolen. By the almighty power of God the Father thou must come;

by the wisdom of God the Son thou hast neither peace nor quiet until thou hast returned the stolen goods to their former place; by the grace of God the Holy Ghost thou must run and jump and canst find no peace or rest until thou arrivest at the place from which thou hast stolen. God the Father binds thee, God the Son forces thee, and God the Holy Ghost turns thee back. (You must not turn the wheel too fast). Thief, thou must come, † † † thief, thou must come, † † † thief, thou must come, † † †. If thou are more almighty, thief, thief, thief; if thou are more almighty than God himself, then you may remain where you are. The ten commandments force thee — thou shalt not steal, and therefore thou must come. † † † Amen.

A WELL-TRIED CHARM.

Three holy drops of blood have passed down the holy cheeks of the Lord God, and these three holy drops of blood are placed before the touchhole. As surely as our dear lady was pure from all men, as surely shall no fire or smoke pass out of this barrel. Barrel, do thou give neither fire, nor flame, nor heat. Now I will walk out, because the Lord God goeth before me; God the Son is with me, and God the Holy Ghost is about me forever.

ANOTHER WELL-TRIED CHARM AGAINST FIRE-ARMS.

Blessed is the hour in which Jesus Christ was born; blessed is the hour in which Jesus Christ was born; blessed is the hour in which Jesus Christ was born; blessed is the hour in which Jesus Christ has arisen from the dead; blessed are these three hours over they gun, that no shot or ball shall fly toward me, and neither my skin, nor my hair, nor my blood, nor my flesh be injured by them, and that no kind of weapon or metal shall do me any harm, so surely as the Mother of God shall not bring forth another son. † † †. Amen.

A CHARM TO GAIN ADVANTAGE OF A MAN OF SUPERIOR STRENGTH.

I [*name*] breathe upon thee. Three drops of blood I take from thee: the first out of thy heart, the other out of they liver, and the third out of thy vital powers; and in this I deprive thee of thy strength and manliness.

Hbbi Massa danti Lantien. I. I. I.

A RECIPE FOR DESTROYING SPRING-TAILS OR GROUND-FLEAS.

Take the chaff upon which children have been lying in their cradles, or take the dung of horses, and put that upon the field, and the spring-tails or ground-fleas will no longer do you any injury.

A BENEDICTION FOR AND AGAINST ALL ENEMIES.

The cross of Christ be with me; the cross of Christ overcomes all water and every fire; the cross of Christ overcomes all weapons; the cross of Christ is a perfect sign and blessing to my soul. May Christ be with me and my body during all my life at day and at night. Now I pray, I, [*name*], pray God the Father for the soul's sake, and I pray God the Son for the Father's sake, and I pray God the Holy Ghost for the Father's and the Son's sake, that the holy corpse of God may bless me against all evil things, words and works. The cross of Christ open unto me future bliss; the cross of Christ be with me, above me, before me, behind me, beneath me, aside of me and everywhere, and before all my enemies, visible and invisible; these all flee from me as soon as they but know or hear. Enoch and Elias, the two phophets, were never imprisoned, nor bound, nor beaten and came never out of their power; thus no one of my enemies must be able to injure or attack me in my body or my life, in the name of God the Father, the Son, and the Holy Ghost. Amen.

A BENEDICTION AGAINST ENEMIES, SICKNESS AND MISFORTUNE.

The blessing which came from heaven, from God the Father, when the true living Son was born, be with me at all times; the blessing which God spoke over the whole human race, be with me always. The holy cross of God, as long and as broad as the one upon which God suffered his blessed, bitter tortures, bless me today and forever. The three holy nails which were driven through the holy hands and feet of Jesus Christ shall bless me today and forever. The bitter crown of thorns which was forced upon the holy head of Christ, shall bless me today and forever. The spear by which the holy side of Jesus was opened, shall bless me today and forever. The rosy blood protect me from all my enemies, and from everything which might be injurious to my body or soul, or my worldly goods. Bless me, oh ye five holy wounds, in order that all my enemies may be driven away and bound, while God has encompassed all Christendom. In this shall assist me God the Father, the Son and the Holy

Ghost. Amen. Thus must I [N.] be blessed as well and as valid as the cup and the wine, and the true, living bread which Jesus gave his disciples on the evening of Maunday Thursday. All those that hate you must be silent before me; their hearts are dead in regard to me; and their tongues are mute, so that they are not at all able to inflict the least injury upon me, or my house, or my premises: And likewise, all those who intend attacking and wounding me with their arms and weapons shall be defenceless, weak and conquered before me. In this shall assist me the holy power of God, which can make all arms or weapons of no avail. All this in the name of God the Father, the Son, and the Holy Ghost. Amen.

THE TALISMAN.

It is said that anyone going out hunting and carrying it in his game-bag, cannot but shoot something worth while and bring it home.

An old hermit once found an old, lame huntsman in a forest, lying beside the road and weeping. The hermit asked him the cause of his dejection. "Ah me, thou man of God, I am a poor, unfortunate being; I must annually furnish my lord with as many deer, and hares, and partridges, as a young and healthy huntsman could hunt up, or else I will be discharged from my office; now I am old and lame; besides game is getting scarce, and I cannot follow it up as I ought to; and I know not what will become of me." Here the old man's feelings overcame him, and he could not utter another word. The hermit, upon this, took out a small piece of paper, upon which he wrote some words with a pencil, and handing it to the huntsman, he said: "there, old friend, put this in your game-bag whenever you go out hunting, and you shall certainly shoot something worth while, and bring it home, too, yet be careful to shoot no more than you necessarily need, nor to communicate it to anyone that might misuse it, on account of the high meaning contained in these words." The hermit then went on his journey, and after a little the huntsman also arose, and without thinking of anything in particular he went into the woods, and had scarcely advanced a hundred yards when he shot as fine a roebuck as he ever saw in his life.

This huntsman was afterward and during his whole life-
time lucky in his hunting, so much so that he was considered
one of the best hunters in that whole country. The following is what the hermit wrote on the paper:

Ut nemo in sense tentat, descendre nemo.

At precedenti spectatur mantica tergo.

The best argument is to try it.

TO PREVENT ANYONE FROM KILLING GAME.

Pronounce the name, as for instance, *Jacob Wohlgemuth*,
shoot whatever you please; shoot but hair and feathers with
and what you give to poor people. † † † Amen.

TO COMPEL A THIEF TO RETURN STOLEN GOODS.

Walk out early in the morning before sunrise, to a juniper-
tree, and bend it with the left hand toward the rising sun,
while you are saying: Juniper-tree, I shall bend and squeeze
thee, until the thief has returned the stolen goods to the
place from which he took them. Then you must take a stone
and put it on the bush, and under the bush and the stone you
must place the skull of a malefactor. † † † Yet you must
be careful, in case the thief returns the stolen goods, to un-
loose the bush and replace the stone where it was before.

A CHARM AGAINST POWDER AND BALL.

The heavenly and holy trumpet blow every ball and
misfortune away from me. I seek refuge beneath the tree
of life which bears twelvefold fruits. I stand behind the
holy altar of the Christian Church. I commend myself to
the Holy Trinity. I [*name*] hide myself beneath the holy
corpse of Jesus Christ. I commend myself unto the wounds
of Jesus Christ, that the hand of no man might be able
to seize me, or to bind me, or to cut me, or to throw me,
or to beat me, or to overcome me in any way whatever,
so help me. [N.]

☞Whoever carries this book with him is safe from all his enemies, visible or invisible; and whoever has this book with him cannot die without the holy corpse of Jesus Christ, nor drown in any water, nor burn up in any fire, nor can any unjust sentence be passed upon him. So help me. † † †

UNLUCKY DAYS,
TO BE FOUND IN EACH MONTH.

January 1, 2, 3, 4, 6, 11, 12.   July 17, 21.
February 1, 17, 18.   August 20, 21.
March 14, 16.   September 10, 18.
April 10, 17, 18.   October 6.
May 7, 8.   November 6, 10.
June 17.   December 6, 11, 15.

Whoever is born upon one of these days is unfortunate and suffers much poverty; and whoever takes sick on one of these days seldom recovers health; and those who engage or marry on these days become very poor and miserable. Neither is it advisable to move from one house to another, nor to travel, nor to bargain, nor to engage in a lawsuit, on one of these days.

The Signs of the Zodiac must be observed by the course of the moon, as they are daily given in common almanacs.

If a cow calves in the sign of the Virgin, the calf will not live one year; if it happens in the Scorpion, it will die much sooner; therefore no one should be weaned off in these signs, nor in the sign of the Capricorn or Aquarius, and they will be in less danger from mortal inflammation.

This is the only piece extracted from a centennial almanac imported from Germany, and there are many who believe in it.   HOHMAN.

IN CONCLUSION THE FOLLOWING MORNING PRAYER IS GIVEN, WHICH IS TO BE SPOKEN BEFORE ENTERING UPON A JOURNEY.   IT PROTECTS AGAINST ALL MANNER OF BAD LUCK.

Oh, Jesus of Nazareth, King of the Jews, yea, a King over the whole world, protect me [name] during this day and night, protect me at all times by thy five holy wounds, that I may not be seized and bound.   The Holy Trinity guard me, that no gun, fire-arm, ball or lead, shall touch my body; and that they shall be weak like the tears and bloody sweat of Jesus Christ, in the name of God the Father, the Son and the Holy Ghost.   Amen.

APPENDIX.

The following remedy for Epilepsy was published in Lancaster (Pa.) papers, in the year 1828.

TO SUFFERING HUMANITY.

We ourselves know of many unfortunate beings who are afflicted with epilepsy, yet how many more may be in the country who have perhaps already spent their fortunes in seeking aid in this disease, without gaining relief. We have now been informed of a remedy which is said to be infallible, and whch has been adopted by the most distinguished physicians in Europe, and has so well stood the test of repeated trials that it is now generally applied in Europe. It directs a bedroom for the patient to be fitted up over the cow-stable, where the patient must sleep at night, and should spend the greater part of his time during the day in it. This is easily done by building a regular room over the stable. Then care is to be taken to leave an opening in the ceiling of the stable, in such a manner that the evaporation from the same can pass into the room, while, at the same time, the cow may inhale the perspiration of the sick person. In this way the animal will gradually attract the whole disease, and be affected with arthritic attacks, and when the patient has entirely lost them the cow will fall dead to the ground. The stable must not be cleaned during the operation, though fresh straw or hay may be put in; and of course, the milk of the cow, as long as she gives any, must be thrown away as useless. [*Lancaster Eagle*].

A SALVE TO HEAL UP WOUNDS.

Take tobacco, green or dry; if green a good handful, if dry, two ounces; together with this take a good handful of elder leaves, fry them well in butter, press it through a cloth, and you may use it in a salve. This will heal up a wound in a short time.

Or go to a white oak tree that stands pretty well isolated, and scrape off the rough bark from the eastern side of the tree; then cut off the inner bark, break it into small pieces, and boil it until all the strength is drawn out; strain it through a piece of linen, and boil it again, until it becomes as thick as tar; then take out as much as you need, and put to it an equal proportion of sheep-tallow, rosin and wax, and work them together until they form a salve. This salve you put on a piece of linen, very thinly spread, and lay it on the wound, renewing it occasionally till the wound is healed up.

Or take a handful of parsley, pound it fine, and work it to a salve with an equal proportion of fresh butter. This salve prevents mortification and heals very fast.

PEACHES.

The flowers of the peach-tree, prepared like salad, opens the bowels, and is of use in the dropsy. Six or seven peeled kernels of the peach-stones, eaten daily, will ease the gravel; they are also said to prevent drunkenness, when eaten before meals.

Whoever loses his hair should pound up peach kernels, mix them with vinegar, and put them on the bald place.

The water distilled from peach flowers opens the bowels of infants and destroys the worms.

SWEET OIL.

Sweet oil possesses a great many valuable properties, and it is therefore advisable for every head of a family to have it at all times about the house in order that it may be applied in cases of necessity. Here follow some of its chief virtues:

It is a sure remedy, internally as well as externally, in all cases of inflammation in men and animals.

Internally, it is given to alay the burning in the stomach caused by strong drink or by purging too severely, or by poisonous medicines. Even if pure poison has been swallowed, vomiting may be easily produced by one or two wine-glasses of sweet oil, and thus the poison will be carried off, provided it has not already been too long in the bowels; and after the vomiting, a spoonful of the oil should be taken every hour until the burning caused by the poison is entirely allayed.

Whoever is bitten by a snake, or any other poisonous animal, or by a mad dog, and immediately takes warmed sweet oil, and washes the wound with it, and then puts a rag, three or four times doubled up and well soaked with oil, on the wound every three or four hours, and drinks a couple of spoonfuls of the oil every four hours for some days, will surely find out what peculiar virtues the sweet oil possesses in regard to poisons.

In dysentery, sweet oil is likewise a very useful remedy, when the stomach has first been cleansed with rhubarb or some other suitable purgative, and then a few spoonfuls of sweet oil should be taken every three hours. For this purpose, however, the sweet oil should have been well boiled and a little hartshorn be mixed with it. This boiled sweet oil is also serviceable in all sorts of bowel complaints and in colics; or when anyone receives internal injury as from a fall, a few spoonfuls of it should be taken every two hours; for it allays the pain, scatters the coagulated blood, prevents all inflammation and heals gently.

Externally, it is applicable in all manner of swellings; it softens, allays the pain, and prevents inflammation.

Sweet oil and white lead, ground together, makes a very good salve, which is applicable in burns and scalds. This salve is also excellent against infection from poisonous weeds or waters, if it is put on the infected part as soon as it is noticed.

If sweet oil is put in a large glass, so as to fill it about one-half full, and the glass is then filled up with the flowers of the St. Johnswort, and well covered and placed in the sun for about four weeks, the oil proves then, when distilled, such a valuable remedy for all fresh wounds in men and animals, that no one can imagine its medicinal powers who has not tried it. This should at all times be found in a well-conducted household. In a similar manner, an oil may be made of white lilies, which is likewise very useful to soften hardened swellings and burns, and to cure the sore breasts of women.

CURE FOR DROPSY.

Dropsy is a disease derived from a cold humidity, which passes through the different limbs to such a degree that it either swells the whole or a portion of them. The usual symptoms and precursors of every case of dropsy are the swelling of the feet and thighs, and then of the face; besides this the change of the natural color of the flesh into a dull white, with great thirst, loss of appetite, costiveness, sweating, throwing up of slimy substances, but little water, laziness and aversion to exercise.

Physicians know three different kinds of dropsy, which they name:

1. *Anasarca*, when the water penetrates between the skin and the flesh over the whole body, and all the limbs, and even about the face and swells them.

2. *Ascites*, when the belly and thighs swell, while the upper extremities dry up.

3. *Tympanites*, caused rather by wind than water. The belly swells up very hard, the navel is forced out very far, and the other members fall away. The belly becomes so much inflated that knocking against it causes a sound like

that of a large drum, and from this circumstance its name is derived.

The chief thing in curing dropsy rests upon three points, namely:

1. To reduce the hardness of the swelling which may be in the bowels or other parts.

2. To endeavor to scatter the humors.

3. To endeavor to pass them off either through the stool or through the water.

The best cure therefore must chiefly consist in this: To avoid as much as possible all drinking, and use only dry victuals; to take moderate exercise, and to sweat and purge the body considerably.

If anyone feels symptoms of dropsy, or while it is yet in its first stages, let him make free use of the sugar of the herb called *Fumatory*, as this purifies the blood, and the *Euphrasy* sugar to open the bowels.

A CURE FOR DROPSY (SAID TO BE INFALLIBLE).

Take a jug of stone or earthenware, and put four quarts of strong, healthy cider into it; take two handfuls of parsley roots and tops, cut it fine; a handful of scraped horse-radish, two tablespoonfuls of bruised mustard seed, half an ounce of squills, and half an ounce of juniper berries; put all these in the jug, and place it near the fire for 24 hours so as to keep the cider warm, and shake it up often; then strain it through a cloth and keep it for use.

To a grown person give half a wineglassful three times a day, on an empty stomach. But if necessary you may increase the dose, although it must decrease again as soon as the water is carried off, and, as stated before, use dry victuals and exercise gently.

This remedy has cured a great many persons, and among them a woman of 70 years of age, who had the dropsy so badly that she was afraid to get out of bed, for fear her skin might burst, and who it was thought could not live but a few days. She used this remedy according to the directions given, and in less than a week the water had passed off her, the swelling of her stomach fell, and in a few weeks afterward she again enjoyed perfect health.

Or: Drink for a few days very strong Bohea tea, and eat the leaves of it. This simple means is said to have carried away the water from some persons in three or four days, and freed them from the swelling, although the disease had reached the highest pitch.

Or: Take three spoonfuls of rape-seed, and half an ounce

of clean gum myrrh, put these together in a quart of good old wine, and let it stand over night in the room, keeping it well covered. Aged persons are to take two teaspoonfuls of this an hour after supper, and the same before going to bed; younger persons must diminish the quantity according to their age, and continue the use of it as long as necessary.

Or: Take young branches of spruce pine, cut them into small pieces, pour water on them and let them boil a while, then pour it into a large tub, take off your clothes, and sit down over it, covering yourself and the tub with a sheet or blanket, to prevent the vapor from escaping. When the water begins to cool let some one put in hot bricks; and when you have thus been sweating for a while, wrap the sheet or blanket close around you and go to bed with it. A repetition of this for several days will free the system from all water.

The following Valuable Recipes, not in the original work of Hohman, are added by the publisher (1856).

CURE FOR DROPSY.

Take of the broom-corn seed, well powdered and sifted, one drachm. Let it steep twelve hours in a wine-glass and a half of good, rich wine, and take it in the morning fasting, having first shaken it so that the whole may be swallowed. Let the patient walk after it, if able, or let him use what exercise he can without fatigue, for an hour and a half; after which let him take two ounces of olive oil, and not eat or drink anything in less than half an hour afterward. Let this be repeated every day, or once in three days, and not oftener, till a cure is effected, and do not let blood, or use any other remedy during the course.

Nothing can be more gentle and safe than the operation of this remedy. If the dropsy is in the body it discharges it by water, without inconvenience; if it is between the skin and flesh, it causes blisters to rise on the legs, by which it will run off; but this does not happen to more than one in thirty: and in this case no plasters must be used, but apply red-cabbage leaves. It cures dropsy in pregnant women, without injury to the mother or child. It also alleviates asthma, consumption and disorders of the liver.

REMEDY FOR THE LOCK JAW.

We are informed by a friend that a sure preventive against this terrible disease, is, to take some soft soap and mix it with a sufficient quantity of pulverized chalk, so as to make it of the consistency of buckwheat batter; keep the chalk moistened with a fresh supply of soap until the wound begins to discharge, and the patient finds relief. Our friend stated to us that explicit confidence may be placed in what he says, that he has known several cases where this remedy has been successfully applied. So simple and valuable a remedy, within the reach of everyone, ought to be generally known.—*N. Y. Evening Post.*

FOR THE STING OF A WASP OR BEE.

A Liverpool paper states as follows: "A few days ago, happening to be in the country, we witnessed the efficacy of the remedy for the sting of a wasp mentioned in one of our late papers. A little boy was stung severely and was in great torture, until an onion was applied to the part affected, when the cure was instantaneous. This important and simple remedy cannot be too generally known, and we pledge ourselves to the facts above stated."

DIARRHŒA MIXTURE.

Take one ounce tinct. rhubarb, one ounce laudanum, one ounce tinct. Cayenne pepper, one ounce spirits of camphor. Dose, from one to thirty drops for an adult.

SOAP POWDERS.

Take one pound of hard soap, cut it fine, and mix with it one pound of soda ash. This article is much used, and its preparation, we believe, is a "great secret."

TO DYE A MADDER RED.

For each pound of cloth, soak half a pound of madder in a brass kettle over night, with sufficient warm water to cover the cloth you intend to dye. Next morning put in two ounces of madder compound for every pound of madder. Wet your cloth and wring it out in clean water, then put it in the dye. Place the kettle over the fire, and bring it slowly to a scalding heat, which will take about half an hour; keep at this heat half an hour, if a light red is wanted, and longer if a dark one, the color depending on the time it remains in the dye.

When you have obtained the color, rinse the cloth immediately in cold water.

TO DYE A FINE SCARLET RED.

Bring to a boiling heat, in a brass kettle, sufficient soft water to cover the cloth you wish to dye; then add 1½ oz. cream of tartar for every pound of cloth. Boil a minute or two, add two oz. lac dye and one oz. madder compound (both previously mixed in an earthen bowl) boil 5 minutes; now wet the cloth in warm water and wring it out and put it into the dye; boil the whole nearly an hour, take the cloth out and rinse it in clear cold water.

TO DYE A PERMANENT BLUE.

Boil the cloth in a brass kettle for an hour, in a solution containing five parts of alum and three of tartar for every 32 parts of cloth. It is then to be thrown into warm water, previously mixed with a greater or less proportion of chemic blue, according to the shade the cloth is intended to receive. In this water it must be boiled until it has acquired the desired color.

TO DYE A GREEN.

For every pound of cloth add 3½ oz. of alum and one pound of fustic. Steep (not boil) till the strength is out; soak the cloth till it acquires a good yellow, then remove the chips, and add the chemic blue by degrees till you have the desired color.

PHYSIC BALL FOR HORSES.

Cape aloes, from six to ten drachms; Castile soap, one drachm; spirits of wine, one drachm; syrup to form the ball. If mercurial physic be wanted, add from one-half a drachm to one drachm of calomel.

Previous to physicking a horse, and during its operation, he should be fed on bran mashes, allowed plenty of chilled water, and have exercise. Physic is always useful; it is necessary to be administered in almost every disease; it improves digestion, and gives strength to the lacteals by cleansing the intestines and unloading the liver; and if the animal is afterward properly fed, will improve his strength and condition in a remarkable degree. Physic, except in urgent cases, should be given in the morning and on an empty stomach, and, if required to be repeated, a week should intervene between each dose.

Before giving a horse a ball, see that it is not too hard nor too large. Cattle medicine is always given as a drench.

PHYSIC FOR CATTLE.

Cape aloes, four drachms to one oz.; Epsom salts, four to six oz.; powdered ginger, three drachms. Mix and give in a quart of gruel. For calves one-third of this will be a dose.

SEDATIVE AND WORM BALL.

Powdered white hellebore, one-half drachm; linseed powder, one-half oz. If necessary, make into a ball with molasses. This ball is a specific for weed. Two ounces of gargling oil, in one-half bottle of linseed oil, is an effectual remedy for worms in horses and cattle.

ASTRINGENT BALL FOR LOOSENESS IN HORSES.

Opium from one-half to one drachm; ginger, one and a half drachms; prepared chalk, three drachms; flour, two drachms. Powder, and make into a ball with molasses.

MIXTURE FOR ULCERS AND ALL FOUL SORES.

Sulphate of zinc, one oz.; corrosive sublimate, one drachm; spirit of salt, four drachms; water, one pint; mix.

YELLOW WATER IN HORSES.

Take Venetian soap, juniper oil, saltpetre, sal prunella, sweet spirits of nitre, of each one ounce; make it into a ball with pulverized licorice root, and give the horse two ounces at once, and repeat if necessary. If attended with a violent fever, bleed, and give bran mashes; or,

Take a gallon of strong beer, or ale, add thereto two ounces of Castile soap and one ounce of saltpetre; stir, and mix daily of this with his feed.

The following is also highly recommended in a German work:

Take pulverized gentian and calamus, of each one-half ounce; sulphate of potassa, two ounces; tartar emetic, liver of sulphur, and oil of turpentine, one-eighth of an ounce each; mix it with flour and water, and give the above in the incipient stage of the disease.

The dose, if necessary, may be given daily for several days.

A VALUABLE RECIPE FOR GALLS — WINDGALLS IN HORSES.

An intelligent and experienced farmer, rising of seventy years of age, residing in Allen township, Cumberland county, has assured us that the following ointment, if applied two or three times a day, will cure the most obstinate windgalls.

Take one pound of the leaves of stramonium (Jamestown weed) bruised; two pounds of fresh butter or hog's lard, and one gill of the spirits of turpentine; put the whole of the ingredients into a clean earthen crock and place it with the contents over live coals for twenty or thirty minutes, stirring it occasionally: then strain it through a coarse cloth or canvas, and it forms a consistent ointment, with which anoint the windgalls two or three times a day.

Fifty dollars had been offered for the above receipt, so says our informant, who kindly furnished it.

WIND-BROKEN HORSES.

The excellent ball for broken-winded horses, that has made a perfect cure of over seven hundred in less than nine months, after many other medicines being tried in vain.

Take myrrh, elecampane, and licorice root, in fine powder, three ounces each; saffron, three drachms: assafœtida, one ounce; sulphur squills and cinnabar of antimony, of each two ounces; aurum mosaicum, one ounce and a half; oil of aniseed, eighty drops. You may make it into paste with either treacle or honey, and give the horse the quantity of a hen's egg every morning for a week; and afterwards every other morning till the disorder is removed.—[*Montague's Farrier*].

INDEX

TO THE ARTS AND REMEDIES CONTAINED IN THIS BOOK.

INDEX (Concluded).

CPSIA information can be obtained at www.ICGtesting.com
Printed in the USA
BVOW05s1500291113

337719BV00008B/476/A